Barbra Streisand

An Illustrated Biography

© Columbia Pictures Industries, Inc.

© Columbia Pictures, Inc.

Barbra Streisand
An Illustrated Biography

by

Frank Brady

Publishers · GROSSET & DUNLAP · New York
A FILMWAYS COMPANY

Designed by Marcia Ben-Eli
Published simultaneously in Canada
Library of Congress Catalog Card Number: 78-73322
ISBN: 0-448-16534-1
First printing 1979
Printed in the United States of America

Contents

1
When Barbra Was Barbara

Contrary to the self-written biography in the *Playbill* of her first Broadway musical, Barbra Streisand was not born in Madagascar, Rangoon, Zanzibar or any other such exotic land. Barbara Joan Streisand was born on April 24, 1942, on Pulaski Street in the somewhat seedy but colorful Williamsburg section of Brooklyn, New York, a neighborhood of first- and second-generation Jewish immigrants. But despite this rather commonplace beginning, her earliest memories confirm her strong identity as someone apart. Barbara was bald until she was two and claims that this made her feel somewhat like a martian.

The daughter of Emanuel and Diana Streisand, Barbara doesn't remember her father. He died of a cerebral hemorrhage when he was thirty-four; Barbara was fifteen months old at the time. Mr. Streisand was an educator, a teacher of English and philosophy with a Ph.D. from Columbia University. Throughout her childhood, Barbara became increasingly interested in and proud of her father's career, and he was often a topic of conversation, as well as a focus of her thoughts. Years later, on Barbara's autobiographical television special, *My Name is Barbra,* she sang a hymn—"My Pa," from the ill-fated 1965 musical *The Yearling*—to the father she had never really known. She has often stated that her life would have been different, less lonely if her father had lived.

Barbara's relationship with her mother was not ideal. On the same television special, one of her songs mentions a mother who tells her daughter that babies are grown in bottles. Perhaps the song alluded to her own mother, whom she has described as "very simple, non-intellectual, non-theatrical. A very secure person . . . sort of normal."

Without a father, Barbara's childhood was sad and often depressing. The family wasn't destitute, but it was certainly poor. When Barbara was born she already had a brother, Sheldon, seven years old. After the death of her father, her mother spent several years virtually without a social life. The family lived on an uncle's army allotment checks. When the checks ran out, Diana took a job as a bookkeeper. Her small salary kept her family alive, but provided no luxuries. Barbara slept on a sofa in the living room and spent her days in the hallways of the six-story apartment building, amusing herself as best she could and occasionally accepting handouts from neighbors.

People often said that Barbara was much older than her years; in fact, somebody once told her that she was probably "born forty." Life in Brooklyn was tough for any youngster. For Barbara, with her unconventional looks and her shyness, it was especially so. In order to get along, most Brooklyn children in less than comfortable circumstances had to rely on their wits and nerve, swiping candy, books, and school supplies. Barbara was no exception and used her imagination and cunning to their fullest to get by from day to day. Making things up became a way of life for her. Since, for instance, she had never had a doll, she devised one, using a filled hot-water bottle that she dressed in a pink sweater and hat. She spent as much time away from the dreary apartment as possible. When she was four, she often visited the apartment of a friend, Irving, whose parents had a seven-and-a-half inch television set. As Irving's mother cooked stuffed cabbage or sat knitting in the kitchen in the afternoon, the two children watched Laurel and Hardy movies through a magnifier.

She spent her first three years of school at a Yeshiva in Brooklyn, where she gained a reputation for her antics. When, for instance, the rabbi would leave the classroom, young Barbara would yell "Christmas! Christmas!"—an appalling profanity in the circumstances.

She was definitely a loner, and not a particularly attractive one. She has described herself as being both ugly and skinny as a child—the kind that looks ridiculous with a ribbon in her hair. Barbara was so thin, in fact, that her mother refused to let her take dancing lessons, because she was afraid her daughter's bones would break. Mrs. Streisand, however, relented when Barbara was seven, and enrolled her in a small dancing school. Looking back at this period of her life, Barbara has stated that when imagining her adulthood she simply could not see herself married and having children, or having any of the things that make up a normal, happy life.

At seven, she made her debut as a singer, at a local PTA meeting. Although sick all day from a severe cold, she argued with her mother until she was allowed to perform. The applause proved to be her medicine. In the same year, Barbara's mother married Louis Kind, a real-estate dealer of modest success. Barbara didn't care much for her stepfather and soon retreated into a fantasy life that maintained her privacy and made her even more of a loner than she had been. Several years later, in 1951, Barbara's half sister, Roslyn, was born.

Having no dates and few friends, Barbara spent much of her time locking herself in the bathroom for privacy, trying on false eyelashes and reciting television commercials. She also spent hours at a time on her apartment rooftop, singing, smoking cigarettes (a vice she gave up when she turned twelve) and dreaming of becoming a star—not just a successful entertainer—a star. She became, naturally, an avid movie-goer and gobbled up fan magazines like popcorn.

When she entered Brooklyn's Erasmus Hall High School, the atmo-

A proud Barbra went backstage to congratulate her half-sister Rosalyn Kind at the Grand Finale in New York, where Rosalyn, just beginning a successful singing career, was performing to standing-room-only audiences. With them is their brother, Sheldon Streisand.

sphere of fraternities, sororities, and fourteen-year-old couples made Barbara feel even more insecure and shy than before. She avoided her fellow students. After school, she drifted through picture arcades, where, after applying mascara and orange lipstick, she would take pictures, which she thought provocative, of herself. Because she felt different from other girls and wished to draw attention away from what she considered her ugliness, Barbara would invariably wear strange-looking clothing. While her classmates were conforming to the styles of the day, including the fad of shortening their noses, Barbara sought to be different. Thus, despite the fact that she was sometimes teased about her oddly shaped nose, she refused to have it "fixed."

At eleven, she began earning money as a babysitter for a neighbor, Muriel Choy. Within a year, she was working after school in the Choy's Chinese restaurant as a cashier and hostess. Barbara got along very well with the Chinese woman who told her about life and sex. She even taught her some Chinese. Acceptance by a minority group made Barbara feel more secure. It was the world against the Chinese restaurant . . . and Barbara.

That same year, 1952, an incident convinced Barbara that she was meant to be an actress. Her mother had slapped her for something she had done, and Barbara pretended she was deaf for several hours. Her mother believed her, and that convinced Barbara that she had theatrical talent. She began to concentrate more and more on an acting career.

Although the treasures of Manhattan's theaters were only a twenty-minute subway ride away, Barbara never saw the lights of Broadway until she was fourteen, when her mother took her to see *The Diary of Anne Frank*. Barbara was not impressed; she knew she could play every part, and better. She started urging her mother to send her to a summer acting camp in upstate New York. Through her own ingenuity and with the money saved from her job in the Chinese restaurant, Barbara financed the first of two summers at Malden Bridge (near Albany, New York). There she made her acting debut, riding a goat across the stage in *The Tea House of The August Moon*.

When she returned from camp, acting preoccupied most of her waking hours. She began working as an usherette at a well-known Brooklyn movie house, the Loew's King. The movie palace was her retreat and her fantasy world. Barbara remembers that she always wanted to be not the actress but the character—not Vivien Leigh but Scarlett O'Hara. When she ushered someone to a seat, she hid her face because she didn't want anyone to recognize her. She felt, she *knew*, she was going to become famous, and she didn't want anyone, in the future, to remember her as a former usherette.

At fifteen, Barbara became increasingly independent. She took an evening job at the Cherry Lane Theater, in New York's Greenwich Village, moving sets and painting scenery. There, she met director Alan Miller and his wife, Anita. In many ways, they helped to change her life by introducing her to literature and to the fantasy world of the theater. She often babysat for them and while her charge was asleep, she would pore over their many books and listen to a wide range of music on their hi-fi. In her fifteenth summer, Barbara returned to Malden Bridge, to appear in *Desk Set* and *Picnic*.

Back in Brooklyn, life was more tedious than ever. Her stepfather and her mother separated. She remained withdrawn at school and refused to participate in high school theatricals: she felt that she should be working professionally; there was no point in doing amateur productions. For Barbara, Brooklyn became a city of "baseball, boredom, and bad breath." Whereas earlier in her life she had filled her time day-dreaming and scrounging food from the neighbors, now she was seeking the culture absent from her days of smoking on the roof.

Her reading habits, until she was sixteen, consisted mainly of mysteries of the Nancy Drew variety. When she became obsessed with acting, she would visit the New York Public Library and read the dramas of Dumas and other great playwrights, in many of which Sarah Bernhardt and Eleonora Duse had performed. She also read Russian plays and novels. It was at about this time that she heard her first classical music, by Stravinsky.

Barbara began to spend nearly all of her after-school time in Manhattan, reading in the libraries, knocking around in off-Broadway theaters, trying to learn her future craft. To occupy time on the subway, she would write letters to Lee Strasberg, of the Actor's Studio, in which she expounded her theory of acting. She would comment on performances she had seen and explain how the roles should be played. Unfortunately, Strasberg never had the chance to profit from these thoughts of a fledgling actress, because Barbara never sent him the letters—after she wrote each one, she tore it up and threw it away. If Strasberg never benefited from her drama criticism, Barbara did; in effect, she was teaching herself how to act.

During her last year at Erasmus High, Barbara's mother sent her to typing school—a concession to life's exigencies. Mrs. Kind believed her daughter could never make a decent wage by acting. Barbara was too skinny, too unattractive, too odd. Barbara resisted. She grew her fingernails long so that she wouldn't be able to type. She was afraid that if she learned to type, she would inevitably become a secretary. She was determined to be true to herself. She was certain that she had talent, and knew it would go to waste if she allowed herself to be pressured into someone else's preconception of her proper place in society. She knew what she was and what she could do, and she trusted her knowledge of herself to determine what was best for her.

In 1959, Barbara graduated from Erasmus, with a 93% average and a medal for excellence in Spanish. She seems to have had a facility for foreign languages. In addition to Spanish, she was learning Italian on her own and picking up some pidgin Chinese from her friend Muriel Choy. She told acquaintances that someday, when she was rich, she would have tutors come to her house to teach her Greek, Japanese, and other languages.

After graduation, Barbara took a job as a switchboard operator in

Manhattan and studied acting in the evenings. Eventually, the contrast between Manhattan and Brooklyn became more than she could stand. As soon as she had $750 in the bank, she left the land of "baseball, boredom, and bad breath" for good.

Barbara's mother continually opposed her, telling her she had no talent and was unattractive. Perhaps Mrs. Kind's opposition stemmed in part from her own failure to achieve a career on stage. She had studied opera but had found the trip from Brooklyn to Manhattan too wearing and eventually gave up her studies. The failure, coupled with her feeling that show business was perilously insecure, made her antagonistic toward Barbara's ambitions. Ironically, it was partly because of Diana Streisand Kind that Barbara attained her status in the entertainment world. Barbara was determined to prove to her mother that she was more than just skinny, ugly, and untalented. When, at seventeen, she moved to the city, she did so with the intention of showing her mother, her high school classmates, and the world that she would soon be a great star.

Barbra as the indefatigable but good-hearted hooker, Doris, in *The Owl and the Pussycat.*

2
Let Them Come to Me

Movie Star News

Barbara Streisand arrived in Manhattan in the summer of 1959, with a suitcase full of wild, wonderful dreams— dreams about being the world's greatest actress. She was determined to be the next Bernhardt, and was convinced that sooner or later it was all going to happen. She attacked Manhattan as if it were a giant ice cream sundae, and she was the only woman in the world with a spoon large enough to handle the sweet gooey confection. Of course, her first responsibility was to learn her craft. She enrolled in three different acting schools simultaneously, hoping thereby to gather knowledge as quickly as possible. Not wanting any of her teachers to know that she was studying with other people too, she adopted a pseudonym—Angelina Scarangella—which she found in the Manhattan telephone directory. She even had it printed on match covers.

Barbara devoted herself totally to her acting lessons. From her first acting teacher, Alan Miller, she learned not only what to do onstage but also what *not* to do. She absorbed her lessons thoroughly, through practice and through watching the other students go through the exercises. More and more, as she watched and worked, Barbara confirmed her

8

belief that the most important lesson was to trust yourself. She watched students doing a relaxation exercise, in which each student had to stand alone on a stage and be himself. She noticed the tension many of her classmates revealed, the little twitches that betrayed their nervousness, and she knew that those who weren't sure of themselves, who didn't have the self-confidence to simply be what they were, would never become stars; many of them wouldn't even get parts. She determined not to make such a mistake.

Barbara's early days in New York were not unlike those of any other young, aspiring actor in the big city. She lived from day to day, taking odd jobs, living off unemployment insurance, and accepting handouts from friends in the business. She lived for months without a permanent home, carrying a small bundle of clothing with her because she never knew where she was going to spend the night. She had keys to her friends' apartments, and wore them on her belt. Their accommodations were anything but elegant: Barbara slept in offices, on stairways, on the floors of her friends' studio apartments. At one point, she tried carrying a cot around with her.

Whether she was working as a switchboard operator, working as a theater usher, or standing on line to collect unemployment benefits, her thoughts were always on landing a role in a show, any show. She read the theatrical newspapers, such as *Show Business* and *Variety*, religiously, looking for announcements of casting calls, and auditioned for every available part. Applying for one after the other, she found out how tiring and degrading auditioning can be. New York is filled with aspiring actresses, and the producers and casting directors can indulge in the frequently petty selectivity of a buyer's market. Once, Barbara wore an old raincoat and a pair of black tights to audition for a part as a beatnik. Although the part was just a walk-on, she wasn't hired, because she had no experience. This infuriated Barbara, and she lashed out, in rather colorful language at those who had rejected her, informing them that she would never again ask them for work. If they wanted her, they'd have to go to her.

When Barbara lost a job as a switchboard operator in a printing plant, she encountered a problem with the unemployment office. She was supposed to be looking for a job as a switchboard operator. Instead, she looked for acting jobs. When the unemployment office checked and found she hadn't gone to interviews for work as an operator, as she had claimed she had, the office stopped issuing her weekly checks. Now Barbara had to find work, any kind of work, and quickly.

© Columbia Pictures Industries, Inc.

Friends of hers told her about a singing contest at a bar in Greenwich Village. If she won, she would get fifty dollars and perhaps a singing engagement for a week. There would also be free food, and Barbara was hungry—for food, for money, for applause. She decided to enter the contest, even though she wanted to be an actress, not a singer. Because she was so frightened, she arranged a practice session in the kitchen of a friend's apartment to bolster her courage. Barbara's "pre-audition" was not in an ornate theater in front of a famous impresario. She was so nervous she couldn't even face the small group of encouraging friends gathered to cheer her on. So she turned her back to the kitchen audience and sang "A Sleepin' Bee" to the calendar on the wall. When she turned around after singing the song, her friends had tears in their eyes. With that reassurance, she entered the contest.

She won. But this success wasn't what she had been dreaming about. She wanted to be an actress, not a singer. But she hadn't been able to break out of the endless cycle of auditions and into an acting job, and she was prudent enough to recognize that the singing job would at least give her an opportunity to be on stage.

In June, 1960, Barbara made her singing debut at The Lion, a gay bar on Ninth Street, in the Village. Dressed in a feather jacket and wearing bizarre white makeup, Barbara created an uproar in the crowded, smoke-filled club even before she opened her mouth. The boys were ready to rip this exotic, multi-colored creature apart. But when she sang the first line of "A Sleepin' Bee," all were silenced. They sat stunned, disbelieving. No woman could sing with so much feeling, so much clarity, so much passion. Then the crowd went wild. She easily beat out a light opera singer, a pop singer, and a comedian. She seemed beyond competition.

It was all very new to Barbara, who had never even been in a nightclub before. The management of The Lion paid her fifty dollars a week, plus food (she fell in love with the London broil), and soon took her down the street to audition at the classy Bon Soir. On stage, Barbara suddenly realized that she had gum in her mouth; so she took it out and stuck it on the microphone. The audience laughed. Although they liked her singing, it was clear that they also sensed the comedienne in her. They weren't the only ones who noticed that she had talent. Comic Larry Storch, headlining at the Bon Soir at the time of her performance, told Streisand: "You're gonna be a star." And Tiger Hayes's girl friend, who had also caught the act, said: "Kid, you got dollar signs written all over you."

Somewhere between the Lion and the Bon Soir, Barbara dropped the middle *a* from her name, which she had long hated as conventionally spelled. Advisors suggested that she not worry about her first name, but that she change her last name. Barbra listened, then came up with a counter-suggestion: she would drop *all* the letters of her name, and just be called *B.*

"And now, The Bon Soir proudly presents Miss Barbra Streisand, née Angelina Scarangella, from Smyrna, Turkey." Barbra took hold of the microphone with all the confidence of a veteran performer. Singing a sexy, *R*-rated version of "Who's Afraid of the Big Bad Wolf," Barbra stunned her audience. She took music discarded by other performers and turned it into personal statements, expressed in her own emphatic way. To find new music to sing, she often called publishing houses pretending to be Vaughn Monroe's secretary. She would sweetly announce that Mr. Monroe needed some fresh tunes for his act, and would suggest that they send over some complimentary sheet music. Her off-stage acting was generally successful; Barbra's mailbox was usually packed with music.

For singers eager to become known on the nightclub circuit, the Bon Soir was the *de rigueur* place to perform. As word spread about the newest singing sensation, Barbra's $108-a-week engagement was extended to eleven weeks. The patrons who flocked to the basement bistro on Eighth Street were witnessing the emergence of perhaps the greatest female popular vocalist of the twentieth century. Many of them sensed that young Miss Streisand would reach new peaks of stardom. They loved her, each one claiming to have discovered the singer. They offered to buy her drinks. But Barbra, never one to be shy, would inform them that she didn't need drinks, she was hungry. To their surprise, she would often announce that she'd rather have a baked potato, and then would proceed to specify how it should be cooked: well-done, with a soft inside and a crisp crust. For those bewildered by her response she made her instructions even simpler: "I like them burned—ya know?"

It was during the first Bon Soir engagement that Barbra became the actress she had always wanted to be. If she couldn't act in a play, then she'd act her way through each song. Singing, she found, could be even harder than acting. On stage alone, she had no other actors to back her up or to react to her lines. She began to respect the profession that had been her second choice, but she was still not ready to commit herself to it. At the Bon Soir, Barbra met her agent, Marty Erlichman. Today, after seventeen years, they are still together and they still have no formal contract.

After her record-breaking eleven-week engagement, Barbra was invited to audition for an off-Broadway show, *Another Evening with Harry Stoones.* This screwball anything-goes revue was the perfect vehicle for Barbra's theater debut. (Actually, she had made her first theatrical appearance in 1960, in a ghastly production of a play called *The Insects,* at the Jan Hus Theater. She played a butterfly.) In *Another Evening,* Barbra would act in nine sketches, and sing three solos and one duet. The other actors on stage included Diana Sands, later to become the original Doris in the stage version of *The Owl and the Pussycat,* and Dom De Luise, today one of the screen's finest funnymen.

On October 21, 1961, Barbra Streisand made her official off-Broadway theatrical debut in *Another Evening with Harry Stoones,* at the Gramercy Arts Theatre. Unfortunately, one evening was just what it was. The show did not have a second performance. Critics from the *Herald Tribune* and *The New York Times* panned it. Reviews in such papers as *Variety* and *The Village Voice,* however, singled out the unique Streisand talent. "Barbra Streisand is a slim, offbeat, deadpan comedienne with an excellent flair for dropping a dour blackout gag, and she belts across a musical apostrophe to New Jersey with facile intensity," said *Variety.* Michael Smith said in *The Village Voice,* "Barbra Streisand can put across a lyric melody and make fine fun of herself at the same time."

Photoreporters, Inc.

After *Harry Stoones*, Barbra began a lucrative engagement at what was then New York's premiere *boîte*, The Blue Angel. Here was the showcase she needed. The Blue Angel had spawned such talents as Harry Belafonte, Carol Burnett, Dorothy Loudon, Nichols and May, and Dick Gregory. Bobby Short was the featured pianist in the cocktail lounge. At this time, Erlichman scheduled appearances for Barbra on every television talk show he could arrange. Her style of conversation soon hooked everyone's attention. Columnist Pete Hamill described her television patter as "a combination of James Joyce and Casey Stengel."

One evening while Barbra was captivating the Blue Angel audience with her melancholy version of "Happy Days are Here Again," the playwright Arthur Laurents was among the crowd. Laurents, who would later write "The Way We Were," was deeply moved by the performance. At that time, he was about to direct David Merrick's newest Broadway musical, *I Can Get It For You Wholesale*. Laurents decided that there had to be a part for Barbra in the show. When she auditioned, at his request, Barbra's singing delighted composer Harold Rome, and Merrick, the producer, was ecstatic. The part of the wallflower secretary, Yetta Tessye Marmelstein, was Streisand's. There was no doubt about her talent. Later, Rome remarked, "When we heard this kid, she just knocked our ears off. We immediately decided to expand the role."

At nineteen, Barbra was signed to her first Broadway musical contract, at $150 per week. (It was during the tryout of the show that Barbra met and fell in love with Elliott Gould.) Barbra's long-established reputation as a temperamental performer began during the show's pre-Broadway run. In her nightclub act, she could choose her own material and sing the way she wanted; she was her own producer, director, and choreographer. Things were different in the theater: Barbra was not the star of the evening, only a secondary character with a big solo number in the second act. When she went into the show, she listened carefully to the director's instructions, and then she argued. With her innate sense of what is right for her, she wanted to do her role *her* way. Lillian Roth, one of the show's stars, appreciated what Barbra was trying to do and tried to help her. But Streisand was independent: she didn't want help from anyone, and she antagonized many people in the show. Even before an audience had a chance to see her in her first Broadway appearance, tempers got so high that Barbra came close to being fired.

I Can Get It For You Wholesale is a musical about the New York garment district during the 1930s. The depression, the idealism, the career opportunism, and the labor unrest of that period were presented in song, dance, and dialogue. During its pre-Broadway run, the show underwent many changes. Barbra's Act II entrance was the subject of many late-night discussions. Finally, someone decided that Barbra should not walk on stage to sing her lament, "Miss Marmelstein." She should enter on a swivel chair with her back to the audience. When she turned around, in a matronly dress and a beehive hairdo, the audience convulsed with laughter. And then she began to sing. Her one solo turn was so memorable that it eclipsed the rest of the show.

On opening night in New York, March 22, 1962, Barbra received an ovation. The show, however, got tepid reviews. John McLain, in the *New York Journal American*, wrote: *"I Can Get It For You Wholesale* could have been called *How to Almost Succeed in Business without Really Being Honest or Very Amusing, For That Matter."* But he added, "Barbra Streisand, who plays a secretary and resembles an amiable anteater, has her moment in the sun with Miss Marmelstein." And Howard Taubman wrote in *The New York. Times:* "The evening's find is Barbra Streisand, a girl with an oafish expression, a loud irascible voice, and an arpeggiated laugh. Miss Streisand is a natural comedienne, and Mr. Rome has given her a brash, amusing song to lament her secretarial fate." John Chapman, in the New York *Daily News*, commented: "I couldn't find one character to whom I could give either affection or admiration. Well, I guess there was one—but she is a minor mouse in the story. She is a harried, frantic, put-upon homely frump of a secretary, and she is hilariously played by a nineteen-year-old newcomer to Broadway, Barbra Streisand." Barbra's boyfriend, Elliott Gould, was barely mentioned in the reviews. Though she loved stopping the show, she worried that it might hurt Elliott.

Barbra's mother came to the opening night but Barbra never felt that her mother appreciated or understood her performance. Whether she was correct or not, her feeling indicates some of the pain and distance between the two women.

During the nine-month run of the musical, Barbra won the New York Drama Critics' award as best supporting actress in a musical; she was also nominated for her first Tony award (she didn't win it). To keep her voice in shape she sang after the show at the Bon Soir. There she could sing the way she wanted, without being tied down to a director's concept of a role.

Barbra had her difficulties through the run of *Wholesale*. Even her biographical sketch, based on information she supplied, in *Playbill* created a minor scandal. The article read: "Barbra Streisand is nineteen, was born in Madagascar and reared in Rangoon, educated at Erasmus Hall High School in Brooklyn and appeared off-Broadway in a one-nighter called *Another Evening with Harry Stoones*. She is not a member of the Actor's Studio." The *Playbill* editors fumed. They demanded the truth about the ingenue's beginnings. A revision was made, which read: "Barbra Streisand is twenty, was born in Zanzibar and reared in Aruba, educated at Erasmus Hall High School." The editors did not appreciate Streisand's peculiar sense of humor. Barbra replied that she'd rather have nothing written about her if she couldn't write it herself. Three months after *Wholesale* opened, an accurate version of the Streisand biography ran in *Playbill:* "Barbra Streisand is twenty, was born and reared in Brooklyn, New York, and educated at Erasmus Hall High School in Brooklyn."

When the curtain came down on *Wholesale*, on December 9, 1962, Barbra didn't have to face the unemployment crisis most actors must deal with when a show closes. Erlichman had already booked her for a tour of the nation's top-rated night clubs. She travelled to Chicago, Los Angeles, San Francisco, and Las Vegas. She was the hottest singer on the circuit and was commanding a salary of $7,500 a week. She was crying a river from coast to coast, touching the hearts of the thousands of listeners who could get to hear and see her in person.

She was also in demand on television, and appeared on the Judy Garland, Bob Hope, Ed Sullivan and Dinah Shore shows. She was winning legions of fans wherever she appeared and even captured the attention of President Kennedy, who, when he saw her appearance on the Dinah Shore show, invited her to perform at a White House correspondents' dinner. She accepted gladly, for she felt Kennedy was a great man. He asked her how long she had been singing, and she answered: ''About as long as you've been President.'' Barbra was less joyful about singing at President Lyndon Johnson's inauguration. She was terribly depressed by the tragedy of Kennedy's assassination and the changes it brought about.

Elliott accompanied Barbra to Los Angeles where she began work in the title role of *Hello, Dolly!*

Authenticated News International

3

Stage and Television

Barbra once told an interviewer: "They tell me I'll eventually win everything, the Emmy, the Grammy, the Tony and the Oscar. It would be beautiful to win all those wonderful awards, to be rich, to have my name on marquees all over the world . . . but I'm living my life one day at a time. And I don't see why it shouldn't always be fun, you know?"

As she played the nation's leading night spots, Barbra began attracting the attention of the music critics of every popular magazine. An early review in *Time,* in 1963, read: "When she sings, everyone knows exactly what she means, even with a banal song she can hush a room as if she really had something worth saying. Barbra seldom hits a note on pitch, but she slides into tune with such grace that her quavers often sound intended. Her style is unmistakably Lena Horne's." In the August 27, 1963, edition of the *Saturday Evening Post,* columnist Pete Hamill described the newest singing sensation as follows: "When she begins to sing, Barbra Streisand suddenly is transformed. Her eyes fixed on some distant point in space, her voice moony, her head cocked to the side, she somehow manages to combine the most engaging qualities of an Egyp-

Barbra rehearsing the play *Funny Girl,* which opened on Broadway on March 26, 1964. Although she was only twenty-one, she had already become a great singer. In her portrayal of Fanny Brice, the public came to appreciate Barbra's talents as an actress and a comedienne.

tian painting and a seductive spook. She has a large voice, rich with nuance, and throbbing with so much feeling."

In December 1963, Barbra Streisand was named Entertainer of the Year by *Cue Magazine*. "Whether it be New York's Blue Angel or Hollywood's Cocoanut Grove, she attracts as many people as the harassed waiters can seat at crowded tables."

For Barbra, the fairly sudden jump to fame was somewhat frightening. The jealousy of less successful performers bothered her. And she missed the spontaneity of her earlier performances at The Lion; now, knowing how much money people were paying to see her, she felt a constant compulsion to make each performance great. Singing was no longer fun; now it was work, very hard work.

Although Barbra created near-riots in her cross-country night club tour, she felt that maybe all those people waiting to hear her were merely part of a cult, a growing group of loyal fanatics. She wanted to, had to, connect with a much larger audience. How else could she ever become a movie star? She couldn't count on a cult to purchase really large numbers of tickets. Barbra needed a vehicle to launch her to superstardom. She needed to prove to the critics and to the ticket buying public that she was an actress, first and foremost. Singing was a secondary occupation.

The vehicle that changed her image, that proved her an actress as well as a singer, was *Funny Girl*. It was a new show that had taken years to gestate; Ray Stark had started to plan the show when Barbra was only eleven years old. Now, by coincidence, he had the script right and was ready to cast just when she was ready to take a new step in show business.

Fanny Brice had been the funniest, homeliest comedienne of vaudeville: Baby Snooks to millions of radio listeners, lover of gambler and bon vivant Nicky Arnstein, later wife of showman-composer Billy Rose. Fanny Brice. Barbra Streisand. The part was tailor-made for the actress's talents. The role of Fanny Brice, the starring role in an elaborate, expensive Broadway musical, would be what Barbra needed to propel her career to the heights. She almost didn't get the part. Ray Stark, the former agent of Marilyn Monroe and Richard Burton, was the son-in-law of the late Fanny Brice. He had seen Anne Bancroft in *The Miracle Worker* and had hired her for the leading part in *Funny Girl*. At the show's first rehearsals, Anne's timing for gags was off, and her voice was weak and thin—she was out. A script was sent to Carol Burnett, who returned it with a note: "You need a Jewish woman to play this part." Kaye Ballard fought, unsuccessfully, to land the lead. Then, a friend of Stark's wife remembered Barbra's outstanding performance in *I Can Get It For You Wholesale*. She told Stark that Streisand reminded her of Fanny. Stark tried her out and was impressed. Barbra was hired.

She was exultant, not only because it was a magnificant part that would allow her the opportunity to show what she could do, but because she was certain that she could do Fanny Brice justice. All it required was being true to herself. She had no intention of imitating Fanny Brice's walk or mannerisms, she had never seen Brice perform, and was glad she

Performing "Cornet Man."

Vamping it up to cover her shyness, Barbra, as the young Fanny Brice, listens as Nick Arnstein (Sydney Chaplin) sings "You are Woman, I am Man."

hadn't. But somehow, in a weird way, as she saw clearly and everyone else would come to appreciate later, the essence of Brice and Streisand were similar. Barbra would not imitate Fanny; she would recreate her and make her her own.

Everything was set. Barbra would play Fanny Brice. Sydney Chaplin, the handsome son of the world's greatest comic, would play Nicky Arnstein. The cast also included Kay Medford, as Mrs. Brice; Jean Stapleton, as Mrs. Strakosh; and Danny Meehan, as Eddie Ryan. Out of town, the show was plagued with problems. Critics in Boston complained of the play's saccharine plot. Because Nicky Arnstein was, in real life, rather disreputable, and because Ray Stark's wife, Frances, was the daughter of

Fanny Brice and Nicky Arnstein, Mrs. Stark insisted that her father's character be whitewashed. The role of Arnstein was so altered that he—a playboy and a gambler—could have fit into the Walton family. Scenes were written, rewritten, and then killed. On the road, $30,000 worth of scenery was thrown out the stage door. Composer Jule Stein (*Gypsy, Bells Are Ringing*), and lyricist Bob Merrill *(Carnival)* wrote twice as many songs as were finally used in the show. Garson Kanin, the original director of *Funny Girl,* was fired five weeks before the proposed Broadway opening, and Jerome Robbins was hired to restage the show. The cost of the musical climbed to a record, for that time, $600,000. The date of the opening was rescheduled five times.

During the show's bumpy pre-Broadway tour, Barbra proved she could learn anything, and quickly, as scenes were written and rewritten and new songs added. During this rehearsal period, Barbra found the challenge and the work fun. She'd eat huge meals, usually Chinese food, before going onstage. The more the writer or composer or director changed the show, the more she loved it. They went through forty-one

Wide World Photos

Tammy Grimes, who was starring in *High Spirits*, took a night off to rub noses with a fellow comedienne. Barbra had just given a benefit performance of *Funny Girl* for the Actors Equity Fund.

Right: Many celebrities visited Barbra in her dressing room in London's Prince of Wales Theatre, following her brilliant performances in *Funny Girl.* Sophia Loren was one visitor. The Italian actress was in London making a new film.

different last scenes before settling on one. Rather than complain about the new lines and stage business she had to learn, Barbra found each night an exciting adventure; she enjoyed not kowing what was going to happen next. One night in Boston, her microphone began to pick up police calls; because the mike was hidden in her dress, to the audience it sounded like strange sounds were coming from her breasts.

Ultimately, of course, the show was set. The script became permanent; there would be no new songs, no more line changes. Then, Barbra began to hate the show. She now had to repeat the same lines, sing the same songs, give the same performance night after night, and she felt as if she had received a jail sentence. Whenever she was onstage, she could

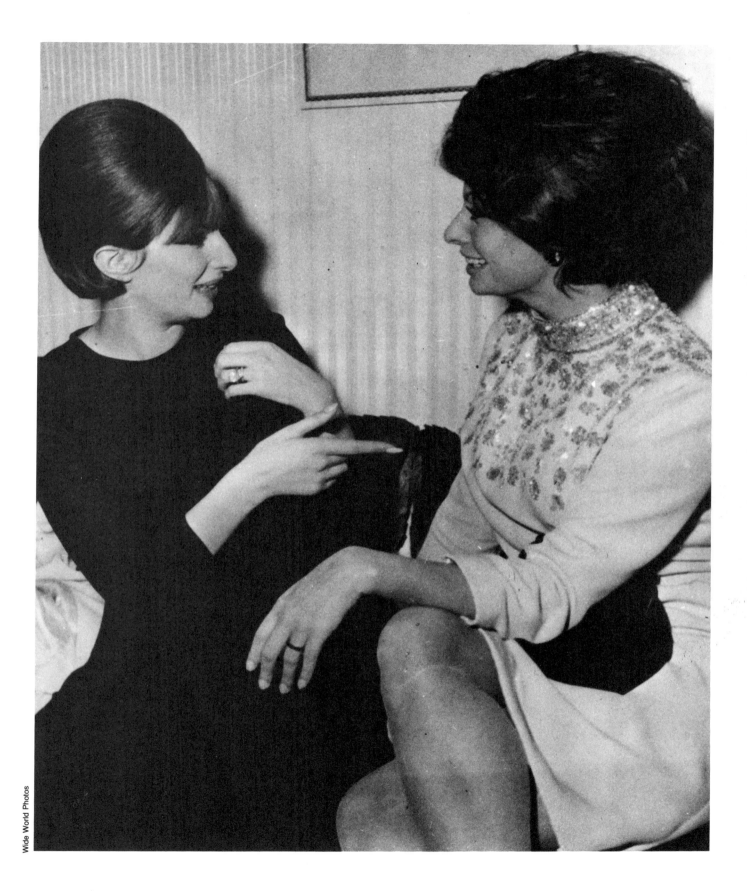

Her Royal Highness Princess Margaret greeted Barbra and her co-star Omar Sharif at the European Premiere of the film *Funny Girl* at the Odeon Theatre in London.

hardly wait for the performance to end. Once, during a particularly tiring rehearsal, the director asked Barbra to do a number over again. Immediately, she exploded and demanded to know *specifically* what she was doing wrong. Stark, from his seat in the audience, said: "Just try it again, Barbra, and then it'll be good." Barbra glared at him and replied: "I didn't come into this show to be good. I want to be great." From that moment on in the show, no one ever told her what to do again.

Opening night at the Winter Garden Theatre, March 26, 1964—the New York premiere of *Funny Girl*. In the opening scene, Barbra sings about being "the greatest star." After the first number, the audience could indeed have felt that she was. They wept during her rendition of "People" and laughed through the hilarious "You Are Woman." When

Barbra belted out "Don't Rain on My Parade," at the end of Act I, the crowd's applause was thunderous. Act II's rousing "Rat tat tat tat," the poignant "Who Are You Now?" and the luminous "The Music That Makes Me Dance" gave the audience more evidence of the astonishing talents of Barbra Streisand.

All that applause, however, did not give Barbra the satisfaction she was seeking. She hated opening night, with the people clamoring around her, trying to buttonhole her, taking her picture, flash bulbs popping. She wanted time and quiet, to think about her performance, for although the audience loved it, she wasn't happy with it. She had signed on to do *Funny Girl* for eighteen months. It would last that long only if it was a hit. Since Barbra generally expects the worst, she wasn't at all sure that the show would be accepted.

The worst did not happen. The critics went crazy. "Magnificent, sublime, radiant, extraordinary, electric," said *Cue Magazine.* In his review in the New York *Herald Tribune* Walter Kerr wrote: "Everybody knew Barbra Streisand would be a star and so she is." *Variety* said: "As it turns out, Miss Streisand is all that the preliminary build-up indicated. She's an impressively versatile talent who clearly has a good future on Broadway, and in the right parts, could also be a bet for pictures."

Barbra's *Funny Girl* performance put her on the cover of *Newsweek* magazine. According to the story of April 10, 1964: "Streisand established more than a well-recollected Fanny Brice. She established Barbra Streisand. When she is onstage, singing, mugging, dancing, loving, shouting, wiggling, grinding, wheedling, she turns the air around her into a cloud of tired ions. Her voice has all the colors, bright and subtle, that a musical play could ask for, and gradations of power too. It pushes the walls out, and it pulls them in. She is onstage for 111 of *Funny Girl's* 132 minutes. Her impact was instant and stunning."

Barbra thought the reviews should have been better. In her typical all-or-nothing excitement, she asked: "All right. What is it? Am I great or am I lousy?" As the show brought record-breaking sums to the Winter Garden, Barbra became increasingly unhappy doing the same part night after night. She fought with her co-star, Sydney Chaplin. Later he was replaced by Johnny Desmond. Barbra was often late and sometimes held up the curtain for twenty minutes or more. When stand-in Lainie Kazan substituted for Barbra for one performance, Lainie got raves from the critics. Barbra, still unsure of her abilities, replaced Lainie immediately. Her performances were uneven—terrific, and not so terrific; intense, and vague. When Barbra's Broadway *Funny Girl* contract expired in December, 1965, she was replaced by comedienne Mimi Hines, who kept the show running for another year.

Barbra's connection with the show, however, was far from over. She was scheduled for a fourteen-week limited run in London's West End, at the Prince of Wales Theatre. The possibility of a movie version and even a sequel was being discussed. She opened in London on April 13, 1966, to the same enthusiastic notices she had received in New York. The show sold out instantly. As European aristocracy began to dine and wine her,

Barbra remained impossibly unpredictable. She made London blush when she met Princess Margaret for the first time. Barbra arrived at a royal gala—late as usual. When she finally greeted Princess Margaret, she apologized for being late: "So sorry, Your Royalty, I got screwed up." Her remark drew a smile from the amused princess, and a loud laugh from Barbra's escort and leading man, Omar Sharif. Her London performance was voted "Best by a Foreign Actress" in a London press poll. During the run of the London show, Barbra announced to an astonished press that she and her husband, Elliott Gould, were expecting a child. A million-dollar concert tour would have to be cancelled so she could have her baby. Barbra was beginning to demonstrate a flair for making headlines.

Although Barbra was nominated for a Tony award for her Fanny Brice portrayal, the award for best actress in a musical went to Carol Channing for *Hello Dolly!* When Barbra's engagement ended in London, so did her professional career on the legitimate stage. She had found the audiences' response gratifying, but doing *Funny Girl* over a long period of time had been tiring, boring, and ultimately an unhappy experience. When it was over, she was convinced she never wanted to do another play. A few years ago, however, Barbra did appear on stage; this time, at the Actor's Studio in a scene from *Romeo and Juliet*. In her estimation, the performance was one of her best. She played Juliet as a spoiled brat, a wealthy, pampered fourteen-year-old who was in love with love, but who knew nothing about life. Barbra emphatized with that conception of Juliet; she, too, used to dream, and cry in her pillow, or even imagine that she was Medea, as she lay in her bed in Williamsburg.

In the early 1960s, Barbra was winning another group to her ever-increasing fan club—the television audience. She first made a big impression as a guest on Mike Wallace's *PM East* talk show, in 1961. In her bizarre clothing, her nonstop, partly nonsensical patter baffled and delighted veiwers everywhere. "Did you see that kooky girl in the funny clothes last night?" was a frequent comment heard after one of her appearances. She was certainly commanding attention. Her manager, Marty Erlichman, booked her on every talk show he could: Johnny Carson, Jack Paar, Mike Douglas. Flip the dial, and there was the skinny Jewish girl from Brooklyn. It was not long before Barbra left the talk-show circuit for the more lucrative and prestigious guest appearances on prime-time variety shows. She cavorted with Dean Martin and Bob Hope on the Bob Hope show in 1963. In the same year, she appeared with Carol Burnett and Robert Goulet on the Garry Moore show, with Georgia Brown on the Dinah Shore Show, and most importantly with Judy Garland on the Judy Garland Show. On the October 6, 1963, appearance with Garland, Barbra and Judy sat together, bar stool to bar stool, both wearing checkered shirts. Barbra sang her heart-rending version of "Happy Days are Here Again" against Garland's up-tempo "Get Happy." The results were sensational. Later in the same show, Ethel Merman joined Garland and Streisand for a roof-blowing version of "There's No Business Like Show Business." Streisand was unquestionably in the same league with these two show business legends.

Right: Barbra's apparent serenity never hinted of the off-camera problems encountered during the taping of her TV special, COLOR ME BARBRA.

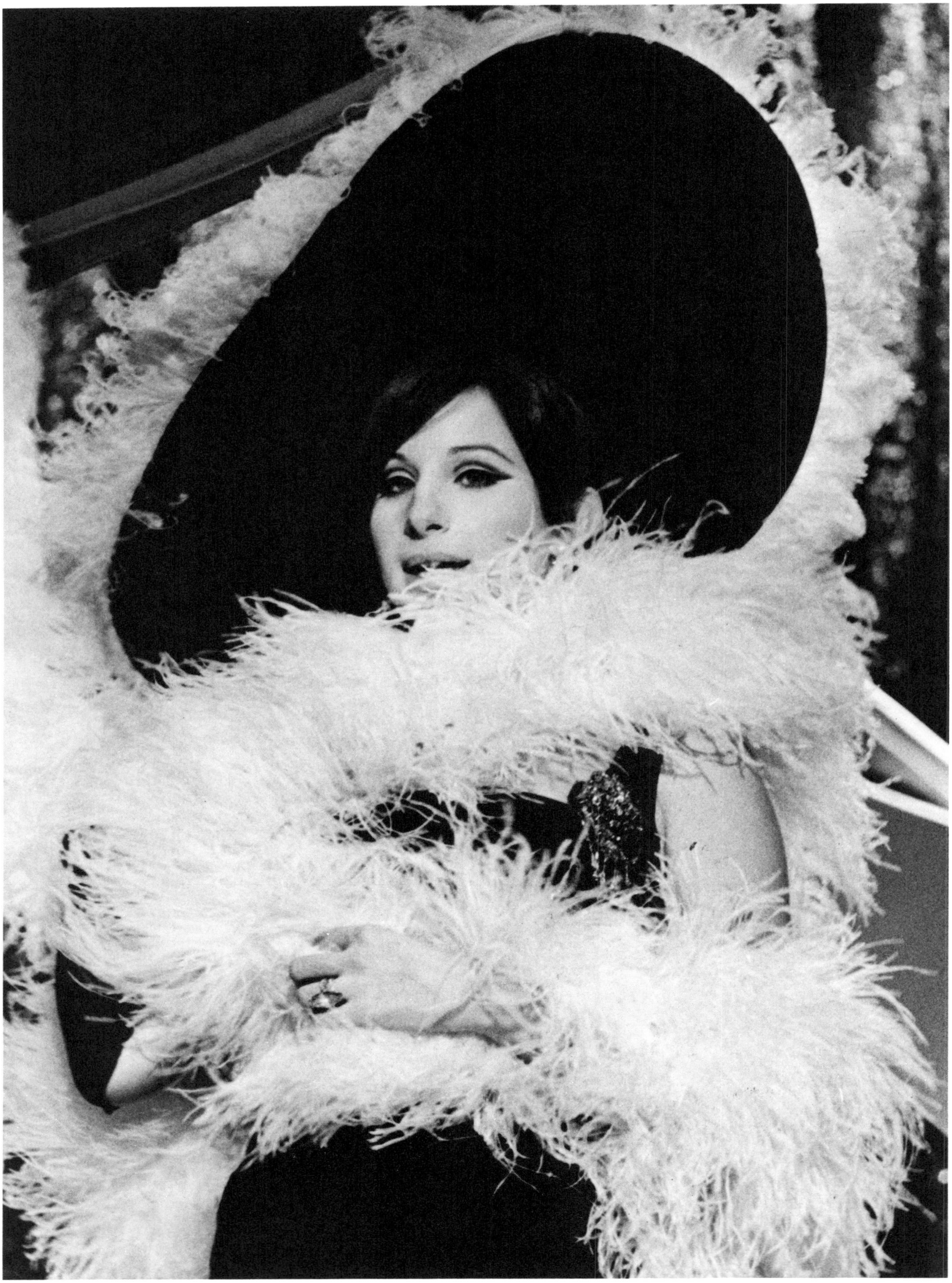

Authenticated News

Television was Barbra's next showcase for her diverse abilities. She was much too good for a few guest appearances a year. She should have her own television show—or at least an hour or two of her own in which to cast her spell on that vast Nielsen family. It was only a matter of time before Barbra signed a contract with a national television network. CBS, after fighting stiff competition from both ABC and NBC, gave Barbra an unprecedented $5,000,000 contract, which permitted her to do as little or as much as she wanted. The most controversial clause of the contract granted Barbra total artistic control of each of her specials. In commenting on the deal perhaps a bit defensively, she admitted that a person should be able to live just as well on $50,000 a year as they could on $300,000.

"My Name is Barbra," her first television special, was aired on April 28, 1965, at 10 P.M. The special was a totally self-revealing musical autobiography highlighting the most significant and sometimes most poignant parts of the young singer's life. She sang songs about the father that she had never known, songs about the joys of childhood, songs about her relationship with Elliott Gould. The most imaginative portion of the program featured an elegantly dressed Streisand romping through the aisles of the exclusive Bergdorf Goodman's department store. Barbra's songs for this segment included: "Second Hand Rose," "Give Me the Simple Life," "I Got Plenty of Nothing," "Brother Can You Spare a Dime," "Nobody Knows You When You're Down and Out," and "The Best Things in Life Are Free."

The critics and the public were shaken and awed by the Streisand performance. *Variety* said: "What counts on television is how the performer projects beyond the glass of the small home screen, and Miss Streisand burst through as though it were no more a barrier than the footlights of a Broadway stage. Her self confidence, especially for her years and one so recently come to stardom, is astounding, and she carries it well. She is destined to hit it big in all media." Barbra's first special picked up five Emmys, including Best Concept, Choreography, and Staging, won by Joe Layton; Best Musical Direction, by Peter Matz; and Best Outstanding Individual Achievement in Entertainment, by Barbra Streisand.

Barbra's first special was shown in black and white and was tastefully and simply produced. *Color Me Barbra,* her second special for CBS, was planned as a far more elaborate affair. The program would use the august Philadelphia Museum of Art for one segment, a live concert for a second segment, and a third segment was to be taped at a zoo, with Barbra clowning around with the animals. The production encountered trouble. The directors of the Philadelphia Museum allowed Barbra and her Ellbar production company sixteen hours for night filming in the museum's stately halls. She would sing as a Modigliani lady, a latter-day Nefertiti, and Marie Antoinette. Famous paintings would complement Barbra and her costumes. But during the filming of the Philadelphia segment, catastrophe struck. Cameras broke. Light cables snapped. Workmen fell asleep from sheer exhaustion. The producers had to re-

Feathers flying, Barbra stars in her third TV special, *The Belle of Fourteenth Street*.

Shakespeare might not have dreamt that his character Ariel could really fly, but Barbra managed it in her TV performance of *The Tempest*.

quest a time extension from the museum. Barbra and her crew worked nonstop for thirty-two hours for the program's art segment, which would eventually be edited to eight minutes. Through the taping Barbra ate: pretzels, peanuts, pickles, stuffed derma, corned beef sandwiches, coffee ice cream. And husband Elliott Gould was there to rub her back and hold her hand between takes.

The experience was exhausting, and left Barbra with the feeling that she would never do a TV series. She found television even more de-

manding than nightly appearances on Broadway. Movies seemed ideal; more than *ever*, she wanted to appear in a film.

The best part of *Color Me Barbra* was Barbra's zoo escapade. She danced with penguins, played Tarzan on the trapeze, and even posed nose to nose with an anteater.

On March 30, 1966, *Color Me Barbra* was shown on the CBS television network. The audience, substantially larger than that for the first Streisand special, was enchanted. In his *New York Times* review, critic

Stage and Television   33

John S. Wilson wrote: "Barbra Streisand's success on her first hour-long special was no lucky accident. She proved that last night when in *Color Me Barbra,* her second annual appearance on the Columbia Broadcasting System, she did variations on the formula of her first show and, if anything, topped herself. In color, the museum settings were magnificent, the circus was happy and Miss Streisand looked gorgeous. It was a fun show."

Barbra's next special, *The Belle of Fourteenth Street,* would recreate an authentic vaudeville entertainment of the early 1900s. This show was remarkably different from each of Barbra's first two specials. She shared the spotlight with several guest stars, including actor Jason Robards, Jr., and song-and-dance man John Bubbles. Barbra and her company came up with the idea of doing a turn-of-the-century variety show, using songs and costumes of that era. It was to be done straight, not as a spoof, but just as variety shows were done then. They researched it thoroughly over a period of months, even calling George Burns for some suggestions and advice. In the show, Barbra did an astonishing eleven-minute quick-change version of *The Tempest* with Jason Robards. She also appeared as the belle of Fourteenth Street, a German lieder singer, a boy soprano, and a stripper. She even sang a number with a pride of plump ladies, all weighing over 200 pounds. Supposedly, those beefy females represented a real singing team who performed in the early days of this century. This $580,000 special was Barbra's first small-screen disaster. Aired on October 11, 1967, the show was panned by the nation's leading video critics. Jack Gould in *The New York Times* wrote: "Barbra Streisand's third television special was an embarrassing outing, a concoction of deranged productions that not even the star and her major colleague of the evening, Jason Robards, could straighten out." Viewers, as well, detested the show. It was never even recorded as a record album.

Barbra Streisand completed two television specials after *The Belle of Fourteenth Street.* On September 16, 1969, *A Happening in Central Park* was telecast. The special featured highlights from Barbra's remarkable concert in New York's Central Park, on June 17, 1967, which was attended by 135,000 fans. Dressed in a rippling, pleated, pink silk dress with a floor-length skirt and a chiffon cape, Barbra sang most of the songs in her repertoire. While she was singing a song from her first ill-fated show, *Another Evening with Harry Stoones,* she forgot the words to "Harold Mengert." A boy in the audience cued her in and got her back on track. The rapport between Barbra and her audience was an appealing phenomenon, even as diluted by a telecast. She closed the concert with a superb version of the Christmas hymn "Silent Night." Again, Barbra had wowed the critics and the audience as well.

Streisand's last television special was not as successful. Filmed during the summer of 1973, *Barbra Streisand and Other Musical Instruments* featured the unusual sounds of over 125 bizarre and exotic instruments. The production was quite a hodgepodge. One minute Barbra would be singing "People" accompanied by Turkish tumbaks, and the next she was singing "Look What They've Done to My Song, Ma" with black singer-composer Ray Charles. There was little of the brilliant Streisand humor in the show; it was loud and loaded with gimmicks. After the show's premiere on November 2, 1973, John J. O'Connor, of *The New York Times,* wrote: "The program is over-produced, over-orchestrated and overbearing to the point of esthetic nausea."

Over the years, she has grown to dislike the world's most popular entertainment medium. Barbra is sickened by the violence that is part of most television shows, and that is even used to introduce the new programs. This particularly disturbs her, because the nightly news is almost the only thing she watches on TV. So she tends to skip the first few minutes, to avoid what she calls the attention-getting "horror stories."

With the exception of a guest appearance on a Burt Bachrach special and an occasional television interview, Miss Streisand has not appeared on television since *Other Musical Instruments,* and at present, there are no television plans on her professional agenda.

4
On Record

The best of Barbra Streisand is on record. In fact, most of Barbra Streisand is on record: Barbra Streisand the actress; Barbra Streisand the antique collector; Barbra Streisand the frightened, insecure child; Barbra Streisand the Broadway belter; Barbra Streisand the comic; Barbra Streisand the sad; Barbra Streisand the jubilant. Listen to just a small sample of any of her many long-playing albums and you'll begin to understand the complexities of this multi-talented woman. For over fifteen years, she has been the number-one female vocalist and recording artist in the world.

Not content to rely on past formulas that have worked well, Barbra has made daring and quite often successful attempts to diversify her style and update her material. Streisand, the singer, always lives in the present. Over the years, she has educated her listeners, taking them on an extended journey of fascinating rhythms and lingering melodies. She is the only contemporary vocalist who can sing the songs of Claude Debussy and Laura Nyro with equal extraordinary skill and total understanding of the material. *Funny Girl* composer Jule Styne has said, "Besides possessing a god-given singing voice, Barbra is the first girl I have ever heard

Streisand's albums immortalized her voice. She has recorded her concerts, film scores, and an immensely varied group of songs, in every conceivable mood and style.

who is a great actress in each song. Barbra makes every song sound like a well-written three-act play performed stunningly in three minutes. At a song's beginning, she establishes her character; next she creates a conflict (making all the lyrics mean so much more than they seem to), then she reaches a tremendous conclusion—so that even after hearing only one song, lasting only a few minutes, one is completely overwhelmed."

The first time Barbra's voice was recorded for the record-buying public was on the original-cast album of Columbia Records' *I Can Get It For You Wholesale,* released in 1962. The biographical note—written by her and drawing on her old fantasy—inside that first album cover reads: "Not a member of the Actor's Studio, Miss Streisand is nineteen and this is her first Broadway show. Born in Madagascar and reared in Rangoon, she attended Erasmus Hall High School in Brooklyn. She appeared Off-Broadway in a one-nighter entitled *Another Evening with Harry Stoones."* The record begins with a brief brassy overture, and then Barbra's voice is heard. The phrasing is perfection and her bell-like qualities come through clearly. The second side of the album features Barbra's show-stopping version of "Miss Marmelstein." But in spite of her remarkable debut on this show record, the album carries all the faults of the Broadway show. The music and lyrics are undistinguished.

Barbra's voice and comedic talent shine through again on her second recording, "A Twenty-fifth edition of the musical review *Pins and Needles,"* written by Harold Rome, composer of *Wholesale.* Like *Wholesale,* the show was about the garment trade. Barbra's voice is the only memorable ingredient on this recording. Whether she's "Doing the Reactionary," singing "Sitting On Your Status Quo" with a chorus, or complaining alone in the spotlight that "Nobody Makes a Pass at Me," Barbra firmly establishes herself on this disk as a singer of great talent.

Those first two records were released by Columbia Records. Eventually, Barbra was offered an exclusive record contract, but only after auditioning for Columbia's president Goddard Lieberson. Although he was interested in her voice and her method of presenting songs, Lieberson wasn't sure that Barbra would be readily accepted by a large section of the public. He thought that the music she sang was much too specialized. When Barbra's first solo album, *The Barbra Streisand Album,* was released in March, 1963, Lieberson was pleasantly surprised to find that his doubts had been groundless. Barbra's first album went to the top of the charts within weeks after it was released. *The Barbra Streisand Album* was a Whitman's sampler of her early nightclub material and included Harold Arlen's "A Sleepin' Bee," a naughty version of "Who's Afraid of the Big Bad Wolf," a melancholy rendition of "Happy Days are Here Again," and a humorous Cole Porter number, "Come to the Market in Old Peking." Barbra, always insecure and self-critical, was embarrassed by this first solo album. She decided that the ending was wrong and that her voice cracked during one song, and she was dissatisfied with the way she had sung "Happy Days." But some of the cuts on this album are excellent. Even Barbra acknowledges that "A Sleepin' Bee" was brilliantly recorded. Her voice was high and thin, and she poured herself

into the song until it re-created her as she had been when she first sang it, years ago. Although it was her favorite song, she never again sang it after that recording.

The second Barbra Streisand album was called just that; *The Second Barbra Streisand Album.* And the material was as eclectic as that of her first album. Jule Styne wrote: "I was one of the early, early Barbra Streisand fans and in all my years of writing songs and being associated with top singers, I have never been as thrilled as I was listening to this new album." With songs like "Any Place I Hang My Hat Is Home," "Who Will Buy?" and "Have I Stayed Too Long at The Fair?" Barbra once again managed to appeal to a broadly based popular audience. This album, too, became an instant best seller.

© Columbia Pictures Industries, Inc.

According to *New York Times* critic Stephen Holden, Miss Streisand's third album, *Barbra Streisand, The Third Album,* has proven to be the most consistent of her early records for quality. "Beautifully arranged in the pop style of the period, with the rhythm supplied only by a bass and drum brushes and background emphasis on strings and woodwinds. *The Third Album* features stunning interpretations of 'As Time Goes By,' 'It Had To Be You,' and 'My Melancholy Baby,' among other standards." A high point of the album is "Just in Time," with an arrangement that

Leonard Bernstein wrote for the wedding of Adolph Green and Phyllis Newman.

Streisand has never been able to decide whether or not she liked her voice. Sometimes she has criticized it for being nasal. At other times, the sound has pleased her, "like a delicate instrument."

Streisand's next album was the original-cast album of *Funny Girl.* Since the album was to be produced by Capital Records, Barbra had to be temporarily released from her Columbia contract obligations. Whether singing "I'm the Greatest Star," "People," or "Don't Rain on My Parade," Barbra's voice on this album has all the energy and excitement of her live Broadway performance. With wonderfully brassy orchestrations, a highly melodic score, and Barbra Streisand's vocal presence, "Funny Girl" is perhaps the most exciting of all Broadway albums. It won a Grammy award for Best Score from an Original Cast of a Show in 1964. In the same year, Barbra won a Grammy for *The Barbra Streisand Album.*

Her fourth solo album, *People,* was released in 1964. John S. Wilson, critic for *High Fidelity* wrote: "Miss Streisand has a kind of authority rare in a popular singer, including the ability to improve on a good performance (a new and excellent version of her *Funny Girl* hit "People" is included here). She has no need of gimmicks, oddities or other crutches. That same skill that made her early innovations seem valid makes these straight presentations just as brilliant." Once again, Streisand's album shot to the top of *Billboard's* Hundred.

Barbra's next three albums, *My Name is Barbra, My Name is Barbra Two,* and *Color Me Barbra,* all contain material from her first two television specials. The largely autobiographical *My Name is Barbra* and *My Name is Barbra Two* feature songs about her youth, her family, her loves. These records are perhaps Barbra's most honest and personal statements in music. *Color Me Barbra* is the perfect memento for fans of her second television special.

Eager to avoid being stereotyped, Barbra made sure her next album was a great departure from her previous ones. In *Je m'appelle Barbra,* she sings in French, and she manages to make it sound like her mother tongue. The liner notes on this album were written by none other than Maurice Chevalier, who appraised her thus: "Barbra Streisand is one of those miracles which come along once in a lifetime, even in America where the sensational apparently never ceases to flourish. She is mad with talent and more gifted than any human being should be permitted to be. She sings 'Les feuilles mortes'—among other songs—with the voice of an angel and gives the French words a poignancy that they have never had before. This very young American girl is enchanting the whole world with an artistry that is new, impulsive and staggering. We bow to you, 'grande, petite Madame.' " Barbra's first composition, "Ma Premiere Chanson," is included on this superb collection of French music.

Barbra recorded *Simply Streisand* and *A Christmas Album* in 1967 and *A Happening in Central Park in 1968.* The soundtrack of Barbra's first film, *Funny Girl,* was also released in 1968.

Barbra puts enormous time and effort into the making of each record, choosing the songs, working on the arrangements and the cover, reviewing and often revising the text that is to go on the record jacket, and editing the recording. Once the album is completed, she claims she never listens to any of it ever again, for fear that she will hear the record's flaws rather than its virtues, and that she'll want to continue working on it to make it sound even better.

Until 1969, Barbra's albums consisted largely of show songs, emotional numbers that she would deliver with her powerful, dramatic force. She had somehow managed to sidestep the music of her contemporaries: Simon and Garfunkel, The Beatles, Carole King. Since Barbra's songs were hardly representative of American music in the late 1960s, in 1969 she decided it was time to catch up. In her album *What About Today?* she sings Paul Simon's "Punky's Dilemma" and the Beatles' "With a Little Help from My Friends." The results were far from successful: the arrangements were too "Broadway," and she appears to have had no talent for contemporary material. Nevertheless, she *did* manage to hit the charts with "Honey Pie," a cut released as a single.

What About Today? was followed in 1970 by the soundtracks of *Hello Dolly!* and *On a Clear Day You Can See Forever. Greatest Hits* contained such classics as "People," "Second Hand Rose," "Don't Rain on My Parade," and "My Coloring Book;" the album set sales records for months.

© Columbia Pictures, Inc.

Her first studio album of the 1970s, *Stoney End,* proved that she could indeed sing contemporary rock and roll with the best of the day's rock artists. The record was produced by Richard Perry, who has also produced albums for Ringo Starr, Harry Nilsson, and Carly Simon. Perry knew what he was doing. Accompanied by standard pop-rock rhythm tracks, Barbra's intelligent renditions of Laura Nyro's "Hands off the Man" and "Stoney End" proved her to be as exciting as any female rock rocalist. Other highlights of the album are Joni Mitchell's "I Don't Know Where I Stand" and Gordon Lightfoot's "If You Could Read My Mind." Rex Reed wrote in *Stereo Review:* "Barbra invests so much energy, discovers so many subtle and fragrant details, and displays so many lyrical attitudes in this program that almost *every* song sounds better that it ever did before."

Barbra Joan Streisand, released in 1971, was also produced by rock wizard Richard Perry. The rock press was not kind to Barbra's work on this album, which included several songs by John Lennon. Stephen Holden remarked in *Rolling Stone,* "An unqualified bummer is Barbra's rendition of John Lennon's 'Mother,' in which she belts out the primal scream." Still, Barbra was making a valid attempt to connect with a younger audience. Her version of Laura Nyro's "I Never Meant to Hurt You" is perhaps the finest version of this song ever recorded.

Barbra's next album, *Live at the Forum,* was recorded at a benefit for Senator George McGovern's campaign for the presidency. With the exception of the real-life element in the album, the record is not very distinguished. *Barbra and Other Musical Instruments* was released in

1973. The record is the soundtrack of Barbra's last television special; both the show and the album were grossly overproduced.

On *The Way We Were,* Barbra sings the title song from the film of the same name. According to *New York Times* critic Stephen Holden: "On this album, Miss Streisand has never sounded more self-assured. Her timbre was darker and her singing altogether more sensual than before. The precociously talented kook now sounded like a grown-up very strong woman." It was the soundtrack to another movie, however, that was to outsell every Streisand album previously recorded. *A Star is Born* has sold nearly five million copies to date, pushing it near the top of the lists of best-selling soundtracks. Although the album was treated unkindly by most critics, Barbra's fans found in it a naive romance that they were seeking. One of the album's songs, "Evergreen," was composed by Barbra herself. The song, with lyrics by Paul Williams, won Barbra an Academy Award. Another contemporary-sounding album, *Lazy Afternoon,* was released during the same year.

In 1976, another facet of Barbra's incredible singing abilities was demonstrated on a long-playing album. *Classical Barbra* is a selection of ten art songs by such composers as Claude Debussy, Carl Orff, George Frederick Handel and Robert Schumann. Leonard Bernstein commented: "Barbra Streisand's natural ability to make music takes her over to the classical field with extraordinary ease. It's clear that she loves these songs. In her sensitive, straight-forward, and enormously appealing performance, she has given us a very special musical experience." Other serious music critics, however, thought Barbra was out of her element. A review in *Opera News* read: "A well-done record for people who like Streisand—not for people who like art songs. This record produces the strange but distinct impression of total lack of rapport between the singer and the rest of the ensemble." The album was a commercial failure.

Barbra has said that for many years she didn't really feel part of the music business, largely because she did not write or compose her own songs. She has an immense regard for those singers who are also talented songwriters, and feels that there may well be more talent in the music field than in films. One difference between the two worlds affected her strongly: the intense, destructive jealousies that are so common to the movie business are, in her opinion, largely absent from the music world, where "everyone in it is functioning at the height of creativity and talent." Apparently the Barbara who sang at The Lion only because she saw it as a way to get a start as an actress has matured into a performer who, through her efforts to improve her craft as a singer, has gained a deep appreciation and respect for all talented musicians.

Butterfly, the first Streisand album produced by Barbra's love, Jon Peters, created quite a stir at Columbia Records. Veteran record engineer Al Schmitt was originally scheduled to produce the album. After Barbra heard three cuts, she said the sound wasn't to her liking. Schmitt was released from the job and Peters took his place. Surprisingly, Peters did a competent job on *Butterfly.* The songs represent a fine mix of reggae, gospel, and contemporary rock. Bob Marley's pulsating "Guava Jelly," Bill Withers' stirring "Grandma's Hands," and David Bowie's weird "Life on Mars" are some of the highlights of this dynamic recording.

Barbra's most recent albums, *Streisand Superman* and *Songbird,* have both been popular with a wide and diverse audience. *Streisand Superman* has sold nearly two million copies to date. A review of her most recent album, *Songbird,* by Dave Blume of the Los Angeles *Times* states: "Streisand's latest album reinforces her status as perhaps America's most acclaimed pop singer but it also supports the argument of those who question her judgment as a record maker. Streisand is singing better than ever. Her sense of soul is beginning to match her mastery of dramatics and vocalese. But it will take a less mundane approach to song selection and considerably less of a conglomerate-type-production effort to lift her to a still-higher plateau of pop glory.''

Barbra claims that she makes no special efforts to care for her voice. Unlike other singers, who exercise their vocal cords by practicing regularly, Barbra only sings when she wants to, and uses no humidifiers or medication to keep her throat in good condition. Instead, she claims she pays no special attention to it at all. She acknowledges that her voice is unique, and attributes its special qualities to her deviated septum. "If I ever had my nose fixed," she has asserted, "it would ruin my career."

Barbra has been producing recordings faster than you can say Angelina Scarangella. And there are sure to be more diverse albums coming from the Streisand voice in the future. For a major portion of the past decade, Barbra has been preparing an album called "Life Cycle of a Woman." She says she has since cancelled the project even though many songs for the album have been recorded. She believes that the concept is a terrific one, but it has so far proven too difficult to execute.

Looking back over her singing career, Barbra is now less critical of herself, more able to accept praise and appreciate her own work. She has even come to like her voice, agreeing with those music critics who point out that while it is less high, it is now richer, producing a warmer, mellower sound. Oddly enough, now that much of her audience thinks of her as an actress—who happens, also, to be a singer— Streisand's singing has become, in some ways, even better than when she first stood before a microphone.

Wide World Photos

5

A Screen Gem

To Barbara Joan Streisand, real fame meant being a movie star. For the skinny kid with the bumpy nose, the rooftops of Brooklyn were the backlots of MGM, RKO, Fox, Warner Brothers—all the major Hollywood studios were found within her landscape. The movie stars were there too: Hepburn, Leigh, Bacall, Mae West. As an usherette at the Loew's King, she studied them, memorized their characterizations, and acted out their roles for millions of imaginary fans. She heard the applause. One day the actual applause would be deafening—Barbra Steisand would become the number-one female box-office attraction in the world.

By 1967 Barbra Streisand had received great acclaim as a stage, television, and recording artist. But at twenty-five, Barbra had yet to make a movie, and she wanted more than anything else to become a movie star. In the early 1960s, however, Hollywood could not accept Streisand. Her looks were unconventional, at best; her name was harsh; her voice was nasal; and her figure was less than Monroe's. Hollywood was no place for an aggressive singer from Brooklyn.

Hollywood is always ready to cash in on a sure bet, however. When

Barbra as the young Fanny Brice, still a youngster in Brooklyn, dreaming of becoming a star.

critics depleted every affirmative adjective in English to describe Streisand's performance in the Broadway production of *Funny Girl,* Hollywood listened intently. If she could be a big hit on Broadway, on the twenty-one inch screen and on the record player, then perhaps she could also be a smash at the Loew's King. After all, someone had to star in the movie version of *Funny Girl.* Streisand's was the only name mentioned.

In the summer of 1963, negotiations for the movie of *Funny Girl* were under way. Barbra waited, refusing to sign a contract for the studio's first offer. She was fully aware that the studio would realize that her name was indelibly linked with *Funny Girl* and that her value as a performer could only increase with time. Her business acumen served her well. She was paid one million dollars for her film debut, the highest salary ever paid for a first movie. In the next eight years, Barbra would star in nine other movies, many oif which are listed in *Variety*'s fifty top-grossing films of all time. Hollywood frequently congratulates itself for giving the ugly duckling a chance. Barbra herself believes that if she had never fantasized about being an actress, she might not have become one.

Barbra, though she's never played the Hedda Gabler or Juliet of her ambitions, has had a rich variety of characters to portray throughout her film career. She's been a hoofer, a hooker, a matchmaker, a political activist, a Manhattan housewife, a rock star, a college girl, and several assorted kooks. She has proven that she is an actress. Her performances are dazzling tours de force. She can be funny, childlike, fragile, invulnerable, and the epitome of womanhood, all at the same time. One moment she convulses her audience with belly laughs; the next, she increases the sale of Kleenex in the theater lobby. On screen she's made love with some of the greatest male box-office stars of our time: Omar Sharif, George Segal, Ryan O'Neal, Kris Kristofferson, James Caan, and Robert Redford. Streisand the woman, the homely, awkward, ex-rooftop actress, is surprisingly sexy on the screen. In the opening sequence of her first film, Barbra stands in front of a mirror and exclaims, "Hello, gorgeous!" The joke became a self-fulfilling prophecy: she has become one of the cinema's natural beauties.

At first, Hollywood was skeptical. Streisand never even had a screen test, yet she was slated to star in not one but three major film musicals, a genre that had peaked in the late 1940s and early 1950s. In addition to Columbia Pictures' *Funny Girl,* she would also appear in Fox's *Hello Dolly* and as Daisy Gamble in Paramount Pictures' *On a Clear Day You Can See Forever.* Over thirty million dollars of studio money was riding on this lady. Barbra was not about to cheat her investors or her future audience.

She was not in the least bit intimidated by Hollywood, its conventions, or its leaders. Defying some of its basic traditions, she was about to become a movie star even though she had never had her nose fixed, her name changed, or her teeth capped. Her success in maintaining these elements of her individuality gave ample notice, for those who cared to listen, of the force of her will and determination. And those who hadn't noticed them before soon had ample opportunity to observe them firsthand.

When Barbra arrived on the set of *Funny Girl* in 1967, she stirred up tornadoes, the likes of which had not been seen since the days of Bette Davis and Joan Crawford. It was Barbra and three-time Academy Award winner, director William Wyler in the ring. The bell sounded and sparks ignited in the crisp California air. Streisand, the perfectionist, instructed Wyler, the general, about how she should be directed. Wyler was the ideal sparring partner. Greer Garson, Olivia de Havilland, Audrey Hepburn and Bette Davis had all won Oscars under his direction. Wyler controlled Barbra's energies. She needed his strengths, his experience. The result was a volatile but profitable relationship. Barbra has stated that she loved and respected Wyler, and felt he gave her equal respect and affection, and that despite the tempestuous moments, their relationship was very good.

Barbra makes the first cut in the cake celebrating the filming of *Funny Girl*. To her right, wearing glasses, is Herbert Ross, who directed the musical numbers, and other members of the cast and crew.

The press was not kind. They labeled Barbra "temperamental," "unfriendly," and "difficult." As her reputation sent tremors throughout the Hollywood community, everyone wanted to see the legend at work. During the months of shooting, Gregory Peck, Ingrid Bergman, and Marlon Brando visited Barbra on the set. Barbra concerned herself with all aspects of the production. She instructed the cameramen, the costume designers, the lighting director. The director of photography, two-time Oscar-winning Harry Stradling, also received constructive criticism from the novice star. Stradling later remarked, "She wanted everything to be the best, the very best. The same as I do. She's very beautiful, there is something in back of that face."

Barbra is flanked by Paul Newman, left, and Sidney Poitier in New York as they signed incorporation papers for the formation of their own motion picture company, First Artists Production Company, Ltd.

Wide World Photos

50

To be the best in such a complex endeavor required constant effort, concentration, and perseverance. Performing is often difficult and almost always a great deal of hard work, but Barbra drove herself (and, often, those around her) toward perfection, in an effort to gain those magical moments that make a film great. She loved being in front of the camera; she found the whole process as exhilarating as it was exhausting. And although Hollywood wasn't overly friendly to Barbra, she loved her new lifestyle. California, she found, is an excellent place to raise children. The climate was to her liking, and the scenery varied and pleasant. She even loved the food!

There was no doubt that Barbra was a terror in front of the cameras. Off camera, too, she upset Hollywood traditions. Her first big coming-out party (Hollywood style) proved disastrous. Ray Stark, the producer of *Funny Girl,* threw an elaborate bash for Hollywood's brash newcomer. All of Barbra's screen heroes were there. The queen of the evening, however, did not arrive in time for her ball. She was ninety minutes late. She arrived with Elliott Gould, sat down, and left the party in an instant. The Hollywood community was outraged at what they considered to be rude and inconsiderate behavior. Contrary to what the press wrote about her or what party guests gossiped about the next day, Barbra did not leave the party to spite anyone. She was nervous, afraid to meet all of those people who had helped make her childhood bearable. Before the party, the extreme tension had made her dizzy and nauseated. Composing herself with great effort, she came to confront those curious, glamorous people, but in a few minutes she was sick again and had to leave the party. During her months of work on *Funny Girl,* Barbra got the worst press ever given a filmland newcomer—that is, until she worked on *Hello Dolly* in 1968.

Even before she began work on the eight-million-dollar motion picture, the press had already announced that Streisand was the wrong type to play the matchmaking toast of Yonkers, Dolly Levi. Besides, Barbra is much too young, they clucked. Carol Channing should re-create the role; even Ethel Merman would be a better choice. In an interview during the filming of *Funny Girl* Streisand herself admitted at the time that she might not be right for Dolly. "I think the part should be played by someone older. Elizabeth Taylor would be perfect."

Directed by Fred Astaire's favorite dance partner, Gene Kelly, and co-starring the craggy-faced Walter Matthau, *Hello Dolly* became a new battleground for the headstrong leading lady.

Although a *wunderkind* as a dancer, Kelly was ineffective as a director. Steisand did what she wanted. She followed her instincts, largely because Kelly didn't give her strong direction. He found himself unable to control her, and Walter Matthau fared little better. Barbra's relationship with Matthau bordered on the maniacal. If he fumbled during a scene, she screamed, "Learn your lines!" And Matthau retorted: "Don't forget, Betty Hutton used to be a big star in this town, too." Later, Matthau said: "She made me physically ill." Their behind-(and sometimes in-front-of-) the camera feud was one of the most bitter in Hollywood history.

With two motion pictures completed, Barbra's next project was Vincente Minnelli's *On a Clear Day You Can See Forever.* Unlike her previous film experiences, the mood on the *Clear Day* set was relaxed, exciting, and totally professional. She, herself, had chosen Minnelli as the director. During her Loew's King days, she had seen Minnelli's *Gigi* and fallen in love with his romantic vision of life. Barbra also got along well with co-star Yves Montand—so well, in fact, that the columnists were spreading rumors about a possible off-screen affair.

For Barbra, the *Clear Day* role was the meatiest in her burgeoning movie career. In the film, Barbra plays two characters: Daisy, a student who undergoes hypnosis to give up smoking, and Melinda, an English lady of the Regency period dressed in elegant Cecil Beaton gowns. She felt that the two parts were similar to two facets of her own personality, the frightened girl, and the strong woman, and she enjoyed acting out both of them.

After the completion of *Clear Day,* Yves Montand complained that all of his best scenes were cut from the film. The cry was familiar: Anne Francis had made similar protestations after the completion of *Funny Girl.* They both blamed Barbra for the scissors job. She, of course, denied having any responsibility for it, and indeed one wonders whether any actress, especially one so comparatively new to Hollywood, could have had the power to compel a director to omit a fellow actor's good scenes. Still, the charges go on.

In 1969, Barbra Streisand, Paul Newman, and Sidney Poitier formed their own production company, First Artists. This group of talented superstars wanted to work for a company that would give them complete artistic control over their work. They agreed to take no salary, maintain strict budget controls, and receive equal shares of profit from each movie. In 1970, Steve McQueen and Dustin Hoffman also joined First Artists as partners.

When Barbra signed her *Funny Girl* motion-picture deal with producer Ray Stark back in 1964, she had agreed to star in three other Rastar productions. Stark refused to let Barbra play Fanny Brice unless he could tie her to a more lucrative contract. Barbra's second movie for Rastar was *The Owl and the Pussycat,* directed by Herbert Ross and co-starring George Segal, the best male comic actor to come out of Hollywood since Jack Lemmon. Based on the Broadway play by the same name, *The Owl and the Pussycat* gave Barbra her first non-singing role. She used this opportunity to change her screen image, wearing less makeup than she'd used in the musicals, and playing the part without wigs, letting her own long hair swing softly. As the Manhattan hooker Doris, Barbra did have a chance to be more natural than she's ever been on the screen—she had to play her first nude scene. When husband Elliott Gould—from whom she was now separated—heard of the scene, he told the press: "I can't imagine how Barbra can do it, she's so shy. I know she must be nervous about it." Barbra, however, stripped for the camera gracefully, with no outward shyness.

The movie was filmed on location in New York City at the time

Frank Teti

Wide World Photos

Barbra's *Hello Dolly* was about to open. The day of *Dolly's* world premiere, Streisand was hard at work in Central Park shooting a scene with co-star George Segal. In the scene, Segal throws Barbra to the ground, humiliates her, and makes her cry. The scene wasn't working. Streisand, the actress, couldn't cry. Director Ross called for a second take, then a third. She racked her brain and received the proper motivation for the scene: "How can I go to the premiere of one of my movies when I haven't even done a decent day's work on my current film? I'd be guilty." Barbra cried buckets. Not a follower of the "Method" school of acting, Barbra approaches her roles intellectually, thinking through the best way to play each scene, and then doing it.

The Owl and the Pussycat was almost a vacation for the indefatigable Barbra. Big musicals take a long time to complete; most non-musicals can be filmed in less than a year, allowing Barbra to spend more time with the people and things she loved.

Barbra had already starred with Omar Sharif, Walter Matthau, Yves Montand, and George Segal. Her next assignment was opposite another Hollywood superstar, Ryan O'Neal in Peter Bogdanovich's screwball comedy, *What's Up Doc?* Barbra had seen Bogdanovich's *The Last*

On Dec. 17, 1969, *Hello, Dolly!* opened on Broadway. Barbra and co-star Louis Armstrong attended the world premiere of the film.

Picture Show and O'Neal's *Love Story*. She wanted to work with both of them, and she was right. The combination proved winning. During the filming, Barbra—it was said and written—had a brief love story of her own with O'Neal. When the work on the movie was finished, so was their rumored romance.

Barbra's mother also attended the world premiere of *Hello Dolly!*

Frank Teti

After *What's Up Doc?* Barbra took a brief six-month layoff from her movie making. She spent it doing ordinary things that were somewhat neglected during months of arduous filming: she took care of her child, ran her home, saw friends, did errands. In that half year, she was, as she put it, a "nonstar," and she loved it—for a little while.

Barbra's next movie, *Up The Sandbox*, was the initial effort of the First Artists production company. There was no doubt that the role of Margaret Reynolds was the most challenging of Barbra's career. The Jewish girl from Brooklyn had to play a WASP housewife who escaped her fears and boredom by retreating into a world of daydreams. That Barbra could play the part believably was evidence of her growing skill as an actress. Based on a book by Anne Richardson Roiphe, *Up The Sandbox* is Barbra's most personal film. She identified with the character of Margaret Reynolds. Although Barbra's own life is very different, she empathized with the frustrations of a life totally limited by the demands of caring for children, keeping house, and cooking meals for her husband. In the film, Margaret Reynolds invents a rich fantasy life to add adventure to her mundane existence. She dreams of blowing up the Statue of Liberty and having an affair with Fidel Castro. Barbra's performance was mature, finely textured, and entirely truthful. But the film, although refreshingly offbeat, had severe editing and continuity problems. It is the one movie of hers that never connected with Barbra's audience.

Barbra still had two movies to complete to fulfill her original contract with Ray Stark. When Stark sent her a fifty page draft of *The Way We Were,* by Arthur Laurents, Barbra thought it would make an excellent film, and immediately decided she wanted to do it. And who would co-star in this serious love story about a Jewish college radical and a handsome conservative WASP writer? The only man in Hollywood who could match Barbra's box office fireworks: blond, blue-eyed Robert Redford would portray Hubbell Gardiner, the man of Katie Morosky's dreams.

Playing a thirties leftist and later an anti-McCarthyite of the 1950s, Barbra was well challenged as a dramatic actress. Not a funny lady, a hooker, or a kook, Barbra's Katie was intelligent, a woman of dynamic ideas. Unfortunately, the plot was no more than a soapy love story— radical Jewish student meets WASP jock writer; radical Jewish lady marries WASP jock writer; radical Jewish woman lose WASP jock writer. But Barbra gave a brilliant performance in *The Way We Were,* possibly the best of her film career. The audience, ignoring the cliches and banalities of the screenplay, loved the Streisand-Redford romance. The movie was a smash.

Barbra was not as fortunate with her next film. *For Pete's Sake,* a popcorn movie suitable for drive-ins and second features, is unquestionably the worst in the Streisand film portfolio. Portraying a kooky (there's that character again) New York housewife who is willing to do anything to help pay back her husband's (Michael Sarrazin) debts, Barbra impersonates a hooker, a cattle dealer, and a secret agent. Her acting style was extremely broad and much of her slapstick was sloppy. Her experience with the film was not a complete waste of time, however, for during the shooting, Barbra met her current love, Jon Peters. And the movie, though not treated kindly by the critics, managed to make a tidy sum of money.

Barbra's next movie should have been called *Son of Funny Girl.* As the final movie in her four-film deal with Rastar Productions, she was slated to make the sequel to *Funny Girl.* Barbra did not want to make *Funny Lady* and her performance in the film lacks all the dramatic fire of its predecessor. She has explained the difference between the two movies: "In *Funny Lady,* I was trying to act the character of Fanny Brice. I also sang Jewish songs like she did in real life. In *Funny Girl,* I didn't have to act the character, I *was* the character. Her essence and my essence were very similar. That is a little spooky, you know?"

Like *Funny Girl, Funny Lady* is based on Fanny Brice's unfortunate romances and her fortunate career. In the movie, Fanny is still in love with Nicky Arnstein (played again by Omar Sharif) but she begins a new love affair with the great impresario Billy Rose (James Caan). Fred Ebb and John Kander, who wrote *Cabaret,* penned five new songs for *Funny Lady.* The score also contains several Billy Rose standards, including "It's Only a Paper Moon." The movie was lavish; it was the most expensive Hollywood musical since *Hello Dolly.* The film's finest moments are the spectacular musical numbers with just Barbra and several hundred thousand dollars worth of scenery on the screen. But *Funny Lady* doesn't hold a match to its famous predecessor.

With *Funny Lady* and her Rastar contract obligations completed, Barbra was free to star in her own projects as well as any others that she and Jon felt were suitable to her immense talents. Peters became increasingly involved with Streisand's professional life, and word leaked out that he would either produce, direct, or star in Barbra's next project, a remake of *A Star is Born.* She had originally turned down the script for the picture, but when Jon became interested in it, she reconsidered, then decided that the movie should be made—yet again (there are two earlier versions of the film: the original was made in 1937, and the first remake in 1954). Barbra felt that this story would give her an opportunity to explore the complex relationship between a man and a woman in today's changing society. It would allow her to express her feelings abut being a woman.

Despite the fact that Jon Peters had developed a chain of extremely successful hair salons in California and was a very wealthy businessman in his own right, the gossips insisted on calling him "the hairdresser," and ridiculed his role in Barbra's projects. She refused to pay attention to the press, naming Jon Peters producer of the forthcoming motion picture. She was its exectuive producer. Outwardly, Barbra displayed an offhand self-confidence about the film, claiming she wasn't worried about failing. However, this was her first venture in controlling all aspects of a motion picture, and the project must have been deeply important to her and to Jon.

She originally wanted Elvis Presley to play the male character; she

Right: After seeing *The Last Picture Show*, Barbra wanted to work with young director Peter Bogdanovich. She got her wish in 1972, co-starring with Ryan O'Neal in *What's Up, Doc?* Here Barbra and Peter pose for the camera.

On a merry-go-round with her husband (played by David Selby) and children in _Up the Sandbox._

thought he had untapped talent as an actor, valued his musical ability, and thought the whole experience would help him and his career. Elvis's advisors were skeptical, and ultimately the deal fell through. Streisand and Peters hired singer-songwriter Kris Kristofferson to play the part, and Barbra found him ideal for the role. He is a talented actor, who had given a powerful performance in _The Sailor Who Fell from Grace with the Sea_; he's an accomplished singer and well able to accompany Barbra on the guitar; and he's handsome.

A Star is Born, a First Artists production, took nearly three years to complete. Perfectionist Barbra not only starred in the movie but also edited, dubbed, and scored the film. Her original music for the song "Evergreen" won Barbra a second Oscar.

The film generated an excessive amount of unfavorable publicity.

Kristofferson often went on drinking binges during the shooting. He told his closest buddies that working with Barbra was worse than being in boot camp. Director Frank Pierson publicly denounced Barbra and her boyfriend-producer in *New York* and *New West* magazines, saying "Working with Barbra was a nightmare."

The press continued writing *mauvais mots* about the filming of *A Star is Born*. Barbra fumed. She defended the movie's cost, $6,000,000, calling that a low-budget film by today's standards, and loudly insisted that she had hired Jon because he was an excellent businessman. Working together, they brought the film in on schedule, and, according to Barbra, under budget. Despite the critics' predictions, it quickly became Barbra's most successful film, in many ways.

When *A Star is Born* was shown in preview for a group of influential

New York critics, they hissed, booed, and talked back to the screen. They gave Barbra and her movie the most devastating reviews of her entire career. But the audience was emphatically on Barbra's side. People turned out by the millions to see the movie; over 5,000,000 of them bought the album of the film score; and she received truckloads of supportive letters.

It has been several years since Barbra's *A Star is Born.* Exhausted from the effort she had put into the picture, emotionally drained from the strain of worrying about all phases of a complex film, and hurt by the caustic reviews, she needed time to regain her creative energy. "I want to have the luxury of doing nothing," she has said. "I'd like to take the same energy that I put into my work and put that into my life." Barbra sometimes talks of directing a movie of her own. It is doubtful, however, that she will ever give up her career as an actress. To her, acting represents a kind of immortality, a way to keep herself remembered. The image on celluloid is a way of prolonging her life.

In the future, Barbra will be quite selective when choosing her movie roles as she has been in the past. Over the years, she has flatly refused leading parts in a large number of films including box office bonanzas like *Cabaret, Diary of a Mad Housewife, Alice Doesn't Live Here Anymore, Klute, The Exorcist,* and *The Devils.* Moreover, she wants to get away from providing mere escapist enterainment. Though she doesn't rule out such films, she wants to do more realistic pictures that deal with important social problems.

Barbra has always said, "I'm an actress, not a singer." The truth is, Barbra is an actress *and* a singer.

THE STREISAND FILM SCORECARD

In descending order of box-office earnings, this is how Barbra's movies have fared.***

Title	Gross Earnings
1. A Star Is Born	$37,100,100
2. What's Up Doc?	28,000,000
3. Funny Girl	26,325,000
4. The Way We Were	25,000,000
5. Funny Lady	19,000,000
6. Hello Dolly	15,200,000
7. The Owl and the Pussycat	11,645,000
8. For Pete's Sake	11,000,000
9. On A Clear Day You Can See Forever	5,350,000
10. Up The Sandbox	Under 4,000,000

***As listed in *Variety,* May 17, 1978

Barbra plays a kooky housewife in *For Pete's Sake,* willing to do anything — including becoming a hooker — to get her husband (played by Michael Sarrazin) out of debt.

Funny Girl

The WILLIAM WYLER-RAY STARK Production

people who see **FUNNY GIRL** again are the luckiest people in the world!

Barbra as the young Fanny Brice,
still a youngster in Brooklyn,
dreaming of becoming a star.

Doing "The Roller Skate Rag."

After her first evening with Nick Arnstein, Fanny begins to fall in love and sings "People."

Spoofing the romantic in her first appearance with the Ziegfeld Follies, Barbra sings and dances her well-padded way through "His Love Makes Me Beautiful."

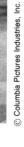

**Here she combines grace with gawkiness
for her own version of "Swan Lake."**

After their marriage, Fanny's thoughts are lovingly filled with Nick.

But work continued, as usual, and Fanny's career flourished.

When Nick sails for Europe, Fanny impetuously leaves the Follies to follow him.

Wearing costumes from *Funny Girl*, Barbra posed for a series of test shootings.

74

Columbia Pictures Industries, Inc.

75

As marital problems grow, even the indomitable Fanny can no longer pretend to be happy.

And finally, there's nothing left . . . except singing.

Hello Dolly

A disgruntled Walter Matthau marches along with the indefatigable Barbra
Streisand in *Hello, Dolly!*

81

A serious moment in an otherwise rollicking musical, which also starred Louis Armstrong.

On a Clear Day
You Can See Forever

Frank Teti

Frank Teti

Director Vincente Minnelli gives Barbra some suggestions during the filming of *On A Clear Day You Can See Forever.*

Barbra, in character, stops to chat with a little boy at the lake in New York City's Central Park.

Right: Streisand and her manager, Marty Erlichman, showed up in old fashioned costumes at a party in Hollywood honoring her for her role in the movie, *On A Clear Day.*

84

85

What's Up Doc?

Ryan O'Neal and Barbra
in *What's Up Doc?*

At the opening party of *What's Up, Doc?* Barbra and director Peter Bogdanovich check out the menu.

Barbra starts to become nervous at being constantly photographed, and complains to Peter.

Then a group of photographers see what's happening, and start coming up from the rear. Barbra finds this all too much to bear.

"I can't stand another flashbulb!" she says to Peter.

Santiago Rodriguez

"Come on, fellas," Peter complains to the photographer. "Give us a break and let us have our dinner."

Tony Rizzo

Ever the gentleman, Peter whips out his handkerchief and does a veronica in front of La Streisand. Privacy at last. Olé!

Barbra sits on a camera seat, waiting patiently for filming to begin.

The Owl and the Pussycat

Columbia Pictures Industries, Inc.

Director Herb Ross (center) supervises a rehearsal on location in Central Park, between George Segal and Barbra, both starring in *The Owl and the Pussycat.*

© Columbia Pictures Industries, Inc.

Segal is amazed to discover Doris playing in a porno film in *The Owl and the Pussycat.*

Doris gets thrown out of even the sleeziest places.

Doris the hooker, ready for trouble.

Barbra did her first nude scene in pictures with Segal in this bathtub tableau from *The Owl and the Pussycat.*

Director Herb Ross (center) intensely discussing a scene with George Segal and Barbra.

Playing Doris in a relaxed moment.

This photo of superstars Segal and Streisand was the principal one used to promote *The Owl and the Pussycat.*

The Way We Were

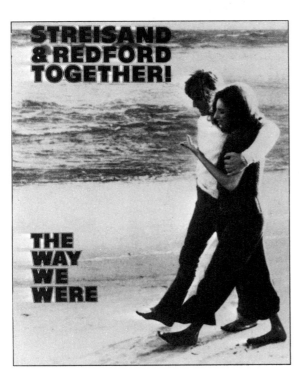

Amidst an enormous exchange of emotional energy, the two great superstars of American movies, Robert Redford and Barbra Streisand, got together in *The Way We Were.*

The unforgettable Groucho visited the irrepressible Barbra, masquerading as Harpo on the set of *The Way We Were*.

Dressed for an outdoor scene in *The Way We Were*, Barbra waits patiently for filming to begin.

In one of the best roles of her movie career, Barbra played Katie Morosky, a campus radical with much talent and great warmth, in *The Way We Were*.

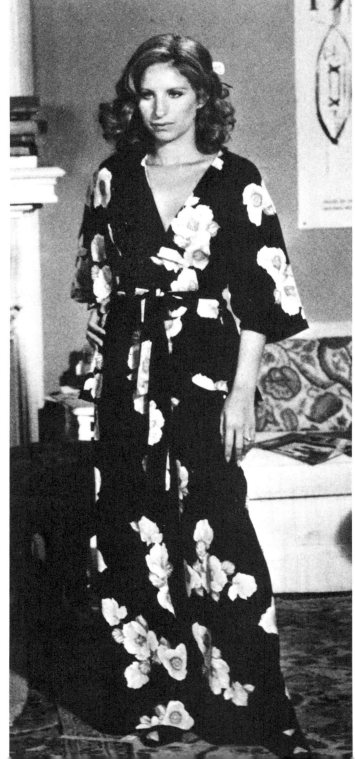

Costume test shootings for
The Way We Were.

The Way We Were became such a popular movie that it influenced fashion in stores all over the country, and Barbra mannequins became a common sight in department stores.

Funny Lady

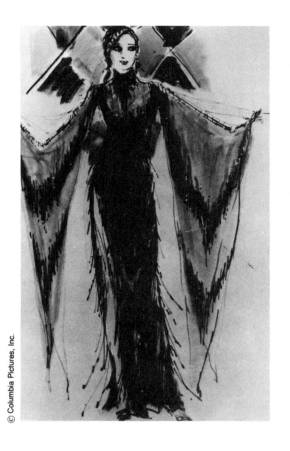

Original costume sketches for Barbra's wardrobe in the film *Funny Lady*.

During one of the most spectacular song sequences in *Funny Lady,*
Barbra wore this award-winning costume. The designer's original
sketch appears earlier.

There were so many costumes and make-up changes in *Funny Lady* that Barbra spent almost as much time in her dressing room (with a battery of dressers, costumers, hair stylists and make-up people) as she did on the set.

Just by sitting in a chair, Barbra, as Fanny Brice in *Funny Lady,* can send audiences into convulsions.

112

United Press International Photo

President Gerald Ford and his daughter Susan attended the premiere and benefit.
After the show, the Fords posed with the stars.

On a trip to Hollywood in 1974, Britain's Prince Charles visited Barbra on the set of *Funny Lady*.

Phil Roach, Photoreporters, In

Fanny Brice played every kind of light comedy and vaudeville role. Here she is ready to go on in Billy Rose's Wild West Show in *Funny Lady*.

In *Funny Lady,* Barbra did a spectacular song and dance number on an elongated cigarette holder.

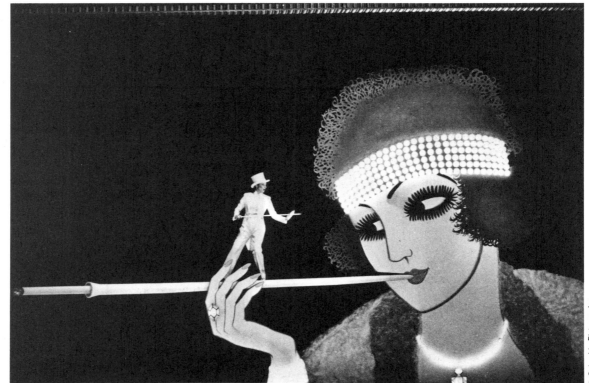

116

The Fanny Brice Show on radio was sponsored by Maxwell House Coffee for many successful years.

Here Barbra does a number with Ben Vereen in *Funny Lady.*

Although she was married to Billy Rose, Fanny always had some room in her heart for her first love, Nick Arnstein.

The love affair between Nick Arnstein and Fanny Brice was perhaps more publicized than the real life relationship between Omar Sharif and Barbra Streisand. Here they are in *Funny Lady.*

118

James Caan played Billy Rose in *Funny Lady*. Here, he and Fanny have a powder-puffing match in her dressing room.

The next week, Barbra and James Caan flew to London, where *Funny Lady* was shown as a Royal Film Performance. Moments before the screening, Barbra and Jim were presented to Queen Elizabeth, along with James Stewart and other film celebrities.

Barbra poses with the crew of *Funny Lady*. Her arm is around the great cinematographer James Wong Howe.

Barbra and co-star James Caan at the Kennedy Center for the Performing Arts in Washington, D.C., for the premiere of *Funny Lady* on March 9, 1975. Streisand and Caan also put on a benefit show for the mentally retarded.

A Star Is Born

The characters played by Kris Kristofferson and Barbra in *A Star is Born* were galvanic, but no more so than their stormy business and creative relationship off the screen in real life.

Barbra holds up her Grammy Award during the 20th Anniversary Grammy Awards ceremonies in 1978. She won the award for best pop performance by a female vocalist, for her rendition of "Love Theme For A Star is Born" (also called "Evergreen"). Barbra not only sang the song, she also composed the music.

Barbra supervised every detail of the making of *A Star is Born*, and the movie was a great box-office success.

Wide World Photos

Her Oscars

Barbra accepts her second Academy Award, but this time it's for composing. She won the Oscar for "Evergreen," the theme song for *A Star is Born*. Neil Diamond, at right, presents the award to Barbra and Paul Williams, who wrote the lyrics to "Evergreen."

Early in her career, columnists were writing that Barbra Streisand would capture every award in the entertainment field: the Tony, the Grammy, the Golden Globe, the Emmy, and most importantly, the Oscar. By 1968, she had attained some of those awards. She had not won a Tony for *Funny Girl* on the stage, but she desperately wanted the Oscar for the screen role. Competition, however, was the stiffest it had been in years: Joanne Woodward, for *Rachel, Rachel;* Katharine Hepburn, for *The Lion in Winter*; Vanessa Redgrave, for *Isadora*; and Patricia Neal, for *The Subject Was Roses*. Joanne Woodward was favored to win; she had already been chosen as the best actress of 1968 by the New York Film Critics. Patricia Neal was the sentimental choice of the Hollywood community.

As the Academy Awards ceremony got under way, no one could be sure who would win the award for best actress. The celebrity-filled audience sat hushed and expectant while Ingrid Bergman opened the envelope. She drew out the card and then, her voice betraying her surprise, announced: "It's a tie!" Two winners had been selected: Barbra Streisand and Katharine Hepburn, Pandemonium broke loose in the auditorium as Barbra, dressed in her skimpy black Scaasi pajamas, ran

Barbra and her first Oscar.

down the aisle. She picked up her Oscar, looked him in the eye and said, "Hello, gorgeous!"

Later, Barbra stated that she thought the Academy Awards selection process was unfair, because "Art has no limits." She pointed out that the year she won the Oscar, there had been five great performances, and all of them should have been honored. Another year, there might be no performances that are really excellent. It's an argument others have made, but the Motion Picure Academy of Arts and Sciences has not yet paid attention to it.

In 1974, Barbra was nominated for her second Oscar. Many of her critics agreed that her performance as Katie Morosky was the best of her career. Indeed, she seemed the number-one candidate. Other actresses nominated were Joanne Woodward, for *Summer Wishes, Winter Dreams*; Ellen Burstyn, for *The Exorcist*; Marsha Mason, for *Cinderella Liberty*; and Glenda Jackson, for *A Touch of Class*. Though Joanne again won the New York Critics Award, the crowd and the Hollywood odds-makers were betting on Barbra. Glenda Jackson, a surprising dark horse, won the Oscar, for her low-key comic performance. Barbra was crushed. She felt that her performance in *The Way We Were* was the best of the five nominated that year.

Barbra has since won a second Oscar, not for acting, but for composing "Evergreen," the theme song for *A Star is Born*. She credits Jon for giving her the inspiration and courage to write the song. Barbra had always wanted to write songs, but wasn't sure she could. Jon reassured her enough to get her to try, and the result was "Evergreen," which has since become a hit recording, gaining Barbra considerable respect in yet another division of the entertainment field.

In future years, Barbra is likely to receive additional Oscars—and not just for performing. Oscars for directing, Oscars for editing, Oscars for scoring; the possibilities are as limitless as her talents.

On April 14, 1969, Barbra Streisand won the coveted Oscar as Best Actress for her role in *Funny Girl*, her first motion picture. At right is Ingrid Bergman, who made the award.

6

Nobody Makes A Pass at Me

The rhetorical question of what could be wrong because no one made a pass at her was warbled in a song with a touch of angst and some defensive humor by Barbra Streisand on the twenty-fifth anniversary edition of the musical review *Pins and Needles*, with music and lyrics by Harold Rome. The recording was made early in 1962, a year when Barbra's luck with men was taking a turn for the better. Before that time, few men *ever* made a pass at the bagel from Brooklyn.

In high school, Barbra never went to a dance, held hands with a boy in a movie theater, or got a good-night kiss at her apartment doorstep. She was pretty much of a loner, and she remembers that she never had a date for New Year's Eve.

Barbra's one high school crush was on the only other kid in school who could match her for eccentricity—Bobby Fischer, later to become chess champion of the world. A year younger than Barbra, he was as much a loner and a character as she. Bobby kept very much to himself, avoiding the other students, often sitting by himself in the school cafeteria wearing earmuffs over his ears, reading *Mad* magazine, and laughing

Bathed in spotlight, Barbra and her husband Elliott Gould attended a party in New York for the opening of her film, *Funny Girl*.

aloud at its jokes. They frequently had lunch together. "I found him very sexy," Barbra once recalled. "You could tell he was a genius, even then. And you know what we talked about? *Mad* magazine."

When Barbra was eighteen she had her first sexual experience, with a young man she met in New York City. "It was terrific and it was terrible," she remembered. "There was no romance." Shortly after that, she met and dated Tommy Smothers of the Smothers Brothers during her first singing engagement outside New York City.

There were no fireworks, no real sparks in Barbra's romantic life until she was nineteen. That year, 1962, she was given an audition for the upcoming Broadway musical *I Can Get It for You Wholesale*. Alone on stage in a scroungy thrift-shop fur, wearing purple sneakers and matching lipstick, Barbra sang a song from her ill-fated off-Broadway show, *Another Evening with Harry Stoones*. The producers asked her to sing another song, and another song, and still another. She topped off the audition with a sizzling rendition of "Too Long at the Fair." The small audience was devastated. Among them was a tall, masculine, dashing young man who had just been signed to play the leading role in *Wholesale*. His name was Elliott Gould, and he sat in the nearly empty theater and listened to the best damned audition he'd ever heard. Barbra sang brilliantly; then she took the opportunity to announce to everyone that her first telephone has been installed that day. She shouted her phone number and pleaded that someone, anyone, phone her, even if it was just to give her the sad news that she hadn't gotten the part.

After the audition, Elliott offered her a cigar. She joined him for a smoke in the dimly lit theater. That night, Elliott gave Barbra a call on her virgin telephone. "You were brilliant," he said, and hung up. The bait was set. And Barbra got the part of Miss Marmelstein, the secretary nobody would ever dream of seducing.

The twenty-three-year-old leading man and the nineteen-year-old cigar smoker began seeing each other. Elliott has said, "She was innocent, vulnerable, afraid. I really dug her. I think I was the first person who ever did."

Their early days together were idyllic. Elliott gave up seeing the beautiful chorus girls that had become so much a part of his life. During the pre-Broadway tour of *Wholesale*, Miss Marmelstein and her leading man were inseparable. When the show finally got to New York City, Elliott moved in with Barbra in her wonderfully bizarre $62.50-a-month apartment of Third Avenue and Sixtieth Street, above Oscar's Salt of the Sea restaurant, The fumes from the restaurant permeated Barbra's apartment. She didn't care. She was in love and already riding on a train of success and critical acclaim.

Barbra's life with Elliott was like nothing she had ever experienced. She was finally celebrating her childhood, twenty years delayed. New York became their playground, their fantastic multi-colored jungle-gym. They spent hours together watching horror movies about gigantic caterpillars and eggplants that eat cities like Pittsburgh and Cleveland. They devoured platefuls of Breyer's coffee ice cream—mountains of it. Late at

Photoreporters, Inc.

night they'd go to Chinatown, where Barbra would draw on her familiarity with Chinese restaurants to order exotic items alien to most Occidentals.

After the brief Broadway run of *Wholesale*, Barbra and Elliott had to devote most of their time to the realities of their careers. Barbra returned to singing, recording her first highly successful album, "The Barbra Streisand Album." By then, she was in demand, jetting off to do the Dinah Shore show in California and playing the major night spots around the country. In March of 1963, Elliott appeared in an unsuccessful production of *On the Town* in London. Their separations brought much tension and unhappiness to them. They wrote each other long, beautiful letters, filled with insights. When Elliott returned to America, his girlfriend was the most famous singer in the country. After a year and a half of living together and apart, Barbra and Elliott were married in Carson City, Nevada, on September 13, 1963.

Money, more money than Barbra had ever dreamed of was pouring in from her work. She was commanding $5,000 a week for her nightclub act, record sales hit the million-seller mark, and she was determined to enjoy her nouveau-riche lifestyle. In their first year of marriage, the

Barbra and Elliott Gould, her leading man in *I Can Get It for You Wholesale* and, offstage, her husband.

Goulds moved into a luxurious apartment on Central Park West, an apartment in which Larry Hart (of Rodgers and Hart) had once lived. The spacious six-room living quarters were adorned with gold records, original Fanny Brice sheet music, autographs and photos of Presidents Kennedy and Johnson, theater signs, and other odds and ends. The furniture was eclectic, found mostly by Barbra during her antique-hunting forays around Manhattan. There were hundreds of used hats and shoes, a lot of stained glass, an old captain's desk, and antique Portuguese chairs. The piéce de résistance, however, was an Elizabethan four-poster of regal proportions. The kitchen was unique, too—it was done in red patent leather. And inside the refrigerator? Matza brie, gefilte fish, kosher salami, caviar, corn fritters, frozen-chicken TV dinners, and gallons of coffee ice cream. Elliott used to go to the floor below their apartment, buzz Barbra on the intercom, and announce: "Come on, time for your chicken soup. It's good for your health."

Unfortunately, the new-found wealth placed a difficult strain on the young couple. According to Elliott, "When success began to come, Barbra and I began to lose something. I don't know what to call it, but the demands on us increased. It was a hard transition to make because we had been together for so long."

As they spent money, they also tried to live simply—a typical Streisand contradiction. Barbra tried living on a twenty-five dollar a week allowance, while at the same time she bought a cream-colored Bentley (she felt it was less obvious than a Rolls). Often, the Goulds would drive it to Snak-time, a junk food restaurant on 34th Street, where they bought thirty-five-cent hot dogs and corn-on-the-cob, and ate them in the back seat.

Barbra's newest success, *Funny Girl,* also put pressure on the already faltering relationship. As Elliott described it, "Our battle was especially difficult because we were real people, not just two profiles or two beautiful magazine covers. We really loved each other." However, they planned to start a family.

Early in 1966, while Barbra was performing in the London version of *Funny Girl,* she announced to an astonished press that she was going to have a baby. The pregnancy meant the Barbra would have to cancel one million dollars' worth of personal appearances.

The press went crazy, dubbing the unborn child the "million-dollar baby." Barbra was annoyed by the emphasis on money; all she was concerned with was the baby's health.

She started to think abut what to name it, and decided that Samantha would be a good name for a girl. (If she became a tomboy, she could be called Sam.) If the baby were a boy, he would be named Jason Emanuel—in memory of Barbra's father, Emanuel.

She discussed her views on child-raising with anyone who would listen. Concerned that her financial success might spoil a youngster, Barbra insisted that her baby would be allowed to enjoy simple things, "like paper, walnut shells," not only expensive toys. She was acutely aware of the need to give a child a strong sense of self-confidence, and to ensure

Wide World Photos

that it would feel loved and wanted.

On December 29, 1966, Jason Emanuel Gould was born, at Mount Sinai Hospital, a healthy seven pounds twelve ounces. Barbra loved the experience of pregnancy; she said she had felt "productive" for nine months, and that the birth of a son gave her a sense of great fullfillment.

While the birth of their son was a pleasure to both Barbra and Elliott, the time spent together was extremely limited. Barbra's new life as a motion-picture actress had just begun. In a few short years, she would star in three major Hollywood musicals: *Funny Girl, Hello Dolly,* and *On a Clear Day You can See Forever.* Because of her intense shooting schedule, Barbra took a house in Beverly Hills, commuting back and forth to New York to be with her husband. Unfortunately, he was not always at home. He, too, had a career, and it was just beginning. He played the lead in Jules Feiffer's *Little Murders* in New York and later had his first true starring role, in *The Night They Raided Minsky's.* Later, he would attain movie star status with an Academy Award nomination for his role in *Bob and Carol and Ted and Alice.*

The two were seeing less of each other than ever before, and their separations were troubled by scandalous accounts in the press of Barbra's alleged affairs. "Barbra and Omar in love," screamed the headlines. Indeed, Elliott *did* have cause to worry. Photographs of Barbra's

Barbra worked throughout her pregnancy. In July, 1966 she arrived at Newport, R.I., with her pet poodle Sady under her arm, to do a one-night appearance at the famous Newport jazz festival.

leading man from *Funny Girl,* with Barbra by his side, were appearing everywhere. She was seen around Hollywood with him and had dinner in his private hotel suite. The nature of their relationship was, however, relatively unimportant because there was by now a truly irresistible rival for Barbra's attention—her work. Barbra became so obsessed with her film career that she lost track of all other parts of her life. Often, however, she took young Jason along with her as she pursued her work.

In January, 1969, columnist Earl Wilson wrote in the *New York Post,*

Jason may not have been brought by the stork, but he got a bit of flying experience rather early in his life when his parents took him to California, where Barbra would soon star in her first film. *Funny Girl.*

"Barbra Streisand and her husband are having marriage problems. The problems are personal and neither will discuss them. But they're further apart now than the mere mileage that separates them." The snowball fights and the coffee ice cream binges were melting away. Then, in February, 1969, Barbra and Elliott issued a joint press statement that read: "We're separating to save our marriage, not to destroy it." Barbra told reporters that she was still madly in love with her husband.

Soon after the separation, Barbra began dating—something she had never really done before. Among other men, she saw a lot of Charles Evans, the dashing brother of Bob Evans, later president of Paramount pictures. She was apparently enjoying her separation.

Later in 1969 another Hollywood couple, Warren Beatty and Julie Christie, split up. Beatty had been a movie idol from Barbra's Loew's King days. When she was in High School in Brooklyn, she had watched him star in *Splendor in the Grass*, with Natalie Wood, and had developed a schoolgirl crush on him, as did many other teenaged girls. Barbra's fantasy came true, though; she and Warren got together for a brief fling, long enough for Hollywood columnists to turn out plenty of copy about the latest film-star romance.

Barbra's love life made great copy not only for American fan magazines, but also for those published in other parts of the world. In 1970, she dated the charming and eligible Pierre Trudeau, the Prime Minister of Canada. When he escorted her to a premier at the Arts Center in Ontario, he gallantly whisked around the limousine to open the door for her.

Trudeau soon asked Barbra to marry him. When she hesitated to give him an answer, he proposed several more times. Barbra, it seems, did love him. Though twice her age, Trudeau is a handsome, intelligent, extremely engaging man. She was enchanted by the thought of being the first lady of Canada, and thought of the exciting changes such a position would bring to her life. She would campaign for Trudeau, become politically involved in all the causes he believed in, and polish up her French until she could speak it fluently. There was only one problem: Canada was too far from southern California. Limiting Barbra's rising career was out of the question, and they both knew their relationship couldn't last with her spending most of her time in Hollywood while Trudeau was in Toronto. They parted as very good friends.

Barbra's next notable escort was Ryan O' Neal, already a box-office star for his role in *Love Story*. Working together under Peter Bog-danovich's direction in the film *What's Up, Doc?* gave them a chance to come to know each other quickly and intensely. Barbra found that O'Neal, like the other men who had been important to her, respected her talent and abilities without being in awe of her. Throughout their relationship, they remained as discreet and as private as possible. But once the intimacy of working together was over, they began to drift apart, and their involvement with each other ended shortly after the movie was completed.

Although seldom without a man by her side, Barbra was not finding the intimacy or the security she had felt with Elliott. Then, in August of 1973, she met Jon Peters. She was filming *For Pete's Sake*, and she summoned Peters, Hollywood's leading hairdresser, to the set to style one of her wigs. "What an insult," he fumed. "I don't do wigs." Barbra has often been criticized for her various hair styles—Rona Barrett acidly commented that one of them looked like "two boxes of steel wool squashed together," and another critic claimed that the real reason Barbra took up with Jon Peters was so that she could have her own

On January 29th, 1970, Canadian Prime Minister Pierre Trudeau escorted Barbra to a party at the National Arts Centre in Ottawa, to commemorate the centennial of the Canadian province of Manitoba. The couple also watched a performance by the Royal Winnipeg Ballet Company.

Wide World Photos

Wide World Photos

In June, 1971, actor Ryan O'Neal escorted Barbra to the Hollywood preview of his film *Wild Rovers*, setting off rumors of a new romance.

Photoreporters, Inc.

"built-in, instant hairdresser" in the house.

Peters was not intimidated by Streisand's talent, because he had reason to believe that he was just as talented in his field. Indeed, Jon Peters, bearded and trendy, had amassed a sizable fortune of his own. His chain of beauty salons in Beverly Hills, Encino, and Woodland Hills grossed more than $100,000 a week. He was also reputedly a notorious Don Juan, whose womanizing was re-created by Warren Beatty in *Shampoo*. Jon, married at the time to television actress Lesley Ann Warren, soon separated from his wife and moved in with Barbra in her magnificent Holmby Hills estate. Half-Cherokee Indian and half-Italian, he had the temper and the stubbornness to match Barbra's. He soon quit his hairdressing business to become her producer and her new image maker. "I didn't fall in love with Barbra independent of her star trip," Peters has admitted. "I was fascinated by her and, of course, by Hollywood. You could describe our relationship as one of creative reciprocity."

And so it seems to be. With Jon's encouragement and support, Barbra has begun to tackle new areas of the entertainment business, from producing films to composing music. His energy and enthusiasm have helped her tap heretofore concealed wellsprings of her talent, and his ideas activate her creative energies.

Peters began to spend more and more time with Barbra's career projects. He produced her highly controversial record album, "Butterfly."

By the spring of 1975, Barbra and Jon were virtually inseparable.

The name has a special meaning for them. When they first met, Jon had told Barbra that she reminded him of a butterfly, and he gave her a 100-year-old Indian butterfly as a symbolic memento.

For the first time during Barbra's hectic career she began to take life at a leisurely pace. The couple bought a ranch at Malibu. Peters had designed the house, and Barbra furnished and decorated it, searching through antique shops for unusual pieces, and in the process becoming something of an expert. It was fun for her, reminding her of the days she'd hunted through thrift shops in New York when she and Elliott were furnishing their first apartment. Certainly, Barbra seemed to be seeking some of the spontaniety she'd had during her first years with Elliott. She and Jon resisted dining at Chasen's or other exclusive California restaurants. The couple would drive around in her Cougar, looking for ice cream stands. She told the press: "We much prefer MacDonald's."

Nowadays, they spend hours riding horseback through Barbra's beautiful estate, and take long strolls along the Pacific Coast. Barbra is at peace with herself. She is slowing down, she is spending more time with her son, Jason. She talks of reading, crocheting, cooking, going back to school. This is the best time of her life.

Peters had been ready to marry Barbra for several years, but she, it seems, has not been ready to marry him. First, Barbra wants to grow as a person and a mother. Marriage is in the future. Perhaps it will never happen. Barbra doesn't care. She has described herself as the happiest she's ever been—"I'm less afraid."

That May, Jon escorted Barbra to Columbia Pictures' 50th birthday. The celebrity-studded party was shown on ABC's Wide World of Entertainment.

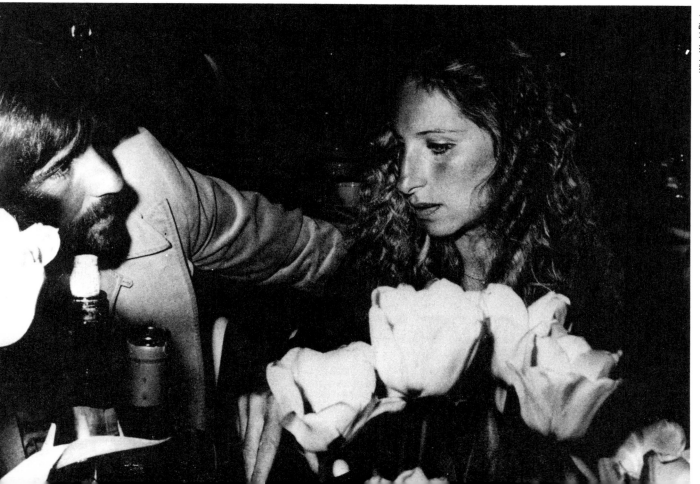

Barbra and Jon Peters left London en route to Paris. The night before, Barbra had been presented to Queen Elizabeth at the Royal Film Performance of *Funny Lady.*

Wide World Photos

7
If a Girl Isn't Pretty

As a child, Barbra Streisand was anything but pretty. She was homely and unattractive, a girl to whom the rest of the children on the block felt superior. "Beak!" "Beak!" they taunted her, insensitive to the pain she felt at their jeering. Barbra remembers that when she was nine years old, the girls in her Brooklyn neighborhood would sometimes gang up on her. They formed a circle around her and made fun of her until she broke free and ran home, crying.

Barbra needed a sense of identity. Too awkward and skinny to ever become a sweet Pollyanna in frilly dresses and lace petticoats, Barbra had to find her own look. She was determined to be unique and beautiful, to make the rest of the world pay attention. But how? One afternoon, she had an inspiration. Barbra, then in her early teens, was riding on the subway with her friend Susan Dworkowitz. Susan had already begun to experiment with makeup, and had used it to make her face chalky white. People stared at her in surprise, totally ignoring Barbra, who sat right next to her. The incident gave Barbra the idea she had been looking for; if she was to stand apart from her schoolmates, she, too, must look different. She decided to cultivate her own style.

At the 1970 Academy Awards, Barbra presented the Best Actor award to John Wayne for his performance in *True Grit*.

142

After the ceremonies, Barbra table-hopped, stopping for a whispered word from Ali McGraw as her husband, producer Robert Evans, listens bemusedly.

Barbra, sporting her new curly hairdo (designed for her by Jon Peters), cuddled bald-pated Yul Brynner when she visited him backstage following his performance in the Broadway play, *The King and I*, in October, 1977.

United Press International Photo

Right: Barbra sang to a packed house in Los Angeles on May 7, 1978, during the taping of "The Stars Salute to Israel at 30". She was one of many Hollywood stars who entertained at the show, which was to celebrate Israel's thirtieth anniversary.

And what style! Barbra began experimenting with her brother Sheldon's drawing pencils. She didn't sketch with them; she used them to color her eyes. Greens, blues, browns, yellows—her face became a living canvas. She found white makeup, and mixed it with her mother's purple lipstick—the result made Barbra's lips a strange shade of violet. One day she bleached the top of her hair, but it turned out an odd blonde color and she didn't like it. She put a rinse on it to change the color, and it did: her hair turned blue and green.

As a teenager, Barbra spent hours in picture arcades, applying different shades of mascara to her eyes and taking sexy photographs of herself. To compensate for her undeveloped figure, she stuffed Kleenex in her bras and panties. The padding wasn't a bad idea; without it, she was pathetically skinny in her long dresses. But the cosmetics certainly made her noticeable as she walked through the halls of Erasmus High. Her classmates nicknamed Barbra "colorful." She generally knew instinctively what was right for her. Experimenting with different clothes, hair styles, and makeup, Barbra sought the combinations that worked best, evolving a style that was hers alone. She thrived on uniqueness.

When Barbra arrived in Manhattan in the summer of 1959, with dyed red hair, white makeup, and green eye shadow, she looked like a grotesque parody of a Christmas tree. Her appearance changed as capriciously as her moods. Sometimes she looked like a typical Greenwich Village beatnik, with black stockings and long hair, and a dirty trench coat tossed casually over her shoulders.

As a money saving device, Barbra began trekking through thrift shops, bargain basements, and antique stores to build up a wardrobe, a necessity for anyone starting out in a career. She didn't like the traditional satin or beaded dresses that many night club singers wore. Instead, she looked for unusual things. For a while, her favorite dress was a simple gingham. She preferred buying offbeat items in thrift shops, paying low prices for uncommon clothing or accessories, and then wearing them only a few times before discarding them, because she tired of things quickly. In her first engagement at the Bon Soir, Barbra appeared in a four-dollar black dress, a two-dollar Persian vest, and old white satin shoes topped by gigantic silver buckles.

Her image as an individualist began to attract attention. Her resistance to current fashion trends, her bargain-basement, thrown-together look, were making serious waves among New York's fashion designers. "This girl is doing it all wrong," they insisted. Yet the clothing, all those feather boas, society castoffs, and ratty fur coats seemed to make sense, at least for Barbra. On one of her first television appearances, in the early 1960s, she told a startled David Susskind, "I scare you, don't I? I'm so far out, I'm in."

When her singing career was firmly established, Barbra began designing her own clothing for her personal appearances. She wandered through stores to see what they were showing, but she claims she found her best design ideas in New York museums. The image of Barbra as the ugly duckling, the beak of Brooklyn, was gone, perhaps preserved only

in her memory. Barbra the young woman, emerging as a powerful performer, was making a fashion statement that was being taken seriously, by her audiences and by the fashion industry itself. And they weren't just commenting about her clothing. This time they were talking about her face, her beauty.

By 1964, the homely kid with the prominent proboscis was appearing on the covers of all the successful fashion magazines. In December of that year, she was in the centerfold of *Vogue,* the quintessential magazine of fashion. The magazine described 1964 as the "wonderful year of Barbra Streisand." The article stated, in part, "No one knows her looks, her odd, compelling beauty the way she does, the length of neck, the slant of eyes, the round of mouth. She knows how to move her arms, her hands with rare grace."

Homely girls and wall flowers all across the United States were begin-

On July 21, 1976, Barbra held a fund-raising party for Congresswoman Bella Abzug, who was seeking the nomination for the U.S. Senate. Barbra jokingly adjusts the large hat that has long been Ms. Abzug's personal trademark. Many movie and television personalities were on hand for the event.

If A Girl Isn't Pretty   147

ning to take pride in their appearances. If Barbra could be beautiful, so could they. When Barbra changed her hairstyle, so did they. A new mascara for the Brooklyn singer? The look was copied by thousands of former plain Janes now out of the closet. What does she eat? What does she read? The girl who was once referred to as an amiable anteater was now Nefertiti. She had broken though the cheerleader stereotype of beauty and had originated her own. Even the most handsome, dynamic men in the world were taking a second look at the new queen of fashion.

What does Barbra Streisand have in common with Gloria Vanderbilt, Charlotte Ford, Mrs. Kirk Douglas, and Rose Kennedy? In 1966, she joined the ranks of these fashionable ladies in being named one of the best-dressed women in the world. In placing Barbra in the highest ranks of fashion, the New York couture group praised Barbra's extraordinary individuality and infallible fashion instinct. Barbra visited the major fashion showrooms of Paris. When she appeared in the Chanel studio dressed in a jaguar-skin suit and matching homburg, even the models stared at her unique style and beauty. She was a woman to be reckoned with, in fashion as well as in entertainment. She was now a sought-after model, and she graced the pages of the world's fashion magazines wearing the plus-ultra chic creations.

In an article entitled "The Girl Who Catches The Light," in the April 1, 1968, issue of *Vogue*, the Barbra Streisand look evoked this appraisal: "She's put svelte and some sulk and a lot of shattering complexity into her version of young fashion individualism . . . and she has scared the wits out of the more rigid fashion individualists as she's made her way. She projects light in a way no other star does, she absorbs it, conserves it, cools it. And Barbra Streisand, the romantic, whose need to be a pretty woman made her a fascinating woman, has stimulated a whole new taste in beauty. The long, expressive perfectly manicured hands, the splendid skin, the shifting smile, the proud nose, they're all part of the irresistible force that powers her style."

Barbra's beauty secrets? For her skin, a beautiful ivory-and-cherry complexion, Barbra uses plain soap and water, but she varies the type of soap according to the condition of her skin. Usually she uses Neutrogena, an extremely mild, nonirritating soap. If her skin gets oily, she switches to an oatmeal soap; if it gets too dry, she uses an apricot soap or one with cold cream in it, along with a mild moisturizer. She likes the idea of pure, natural things.

The once colorful face of Barbra Streisand is now less unconventional. She uses a slight blush on her cheeks, and brown edging on her lips. On rare occasions, she uses a natural-looking makeup base, like Max Factor's "Chinese." Her nails have become a trademark: for years, she wore them very long and beautifully manicured, to set off her slender, expressive hands. During the filming of *A Star is Born*, however, Barbra had to clip her nails to play the guitar. At first, she cut only the nails of her right hand. Then she found that shorter nails enabled her to do things that had been difficult or impossible before. She could garden and cook more easily, and she had to be less cautious about accidently scratching someone. "I could even touch someone's eyes," she realized. "I could also touch my own eyes."

Barbra is very conscious of her weight. She's five feet five inches tall, and generally about 115 pounds. Though she's sometimes as light as 110 pounds, at other times her weight may reach 125, but it is never higher. She doesn't actually diet, and claims that nothing can make her stop eating. She takes only a small breakfast and lunch, but at some point in the day she gets an overwhelming urge to "nosh" on something— usually coffee ice cream with a whipped topping. Her concession to calories? The topping is dietetic.

Exercise is an important part of her health program. In addition to horseback riding, she takes a two-mile walk at least three times a week. Barbra avoids alcohol, which makes her even more unusual in Hollywood society. She dislikes the taste of wine and liquor, but even more

Wide World Photos

importantly, she is afraid of the loss of control that alcohol and other drugs cause. And while she did start to smoke at a very young age, she wisely gave it up, when she was twelve.

The Barbra Streisand of today is far more casual than she was during the early years in Manhattan. The ratty fur coats and feather boas are just dusty memories hidden in a forgotten closet. Barbra wears T-shirts and blue jeans, comfortable shoes, little makeup. She no longer needs a kooky façade to attract attention. Barbra, the natural, cool, contemporary

One of the dream sequences in *Up the Sandbox* was shot in Africa. Barbra took a short vacation during production, and flew the short distance to Israel. Here she dines with Yigal Allon, then deputy premier of Israel.

woman, no longer feels ugly inside. The looking glass and the eyes of millions of adoring fans have told her repeatedly that she is truly a beautiful woman. "The main thing is to go with what you've got," is her attitude. But with her newly earned wealth, she has been known occasionally to go on shopping binges that delight department store managers. On one recent trek through a Beverly Hills clothing store—to avoid the curious fans who always mob her, she had arranged to visit the store after closing time—she went on a wild buying spree, spending some $3000 on twenty-eight pairs of shoes and about $3500 on clothes.

Barbra's sense of style is not limited to her wardrobe or her makeup. She loves beautiful things, on her and around her. She is an outstanding interior designer, using her eclectic tastes to extraordinary effect. Barbra's first New York apartment, the one above Oscar's Salt of the Sea restaurant, was a fascinating mélange of junk and antiques, kitsch and common sense. She took her decorating as seriously as she took her career. When she moved into Larry (Lorenz) Hart's spacious apartment on Central Park West, she used her creative imagination to furnish the rooms with the most elegant antiques available, Wedgwood buckets, stately wooden desks, and Portuguese chairs. The Manhattan residence, with its red patent-leather kitchen, was a showcase.

Barbra's decorating genius has been brought to full flower with the completion of the interior design of her fifty-year-old California estate. The house has been featured in the August, 1974, edition of *House Beautiful* and other respected interior design periodicals. Its style is an exciting mixture of Art Nouveau and Art Deco. In the entrance foyer of her mansion, Barbra has hung majestic portraits of Sarah Bernhardt, by the renowed artist Alphonse Mucha. Throughout the house, there are magnificent textures, sparkling chandeliers, and elegant silver pieces.

Barbra even has a junk room dedicated to sentiment. Many souvenirs from her films are showcased there. The room, like the rest of her home, is representative of Barbra's life—the priceless antiques; the daring blend of diverse designs, periods, and ideas; the dedication to cultivating beauty. Barbra's unerring taste is as evident in all this as it is in her work. Inevitably, she puts her personal stamp on everything she does.

Barbra with her son, Jason, in March, 1972.

151

Frank Teti